W9-ANW-070

Storybook Favorites IN CROSS-STITCH

746.443 $19.95
Sou   Souter, Gillian
           Storybook
           favorites in cross-
           stitch

Free Public Library
Dalton, Massachusetts

First opened, May 1861   Accepted by Town, March 1885

Storybook Favorites

IN

CROSS-STITCH

Gillian Souter

Dutton Children's Books

NEW YORK

746.443
Sou

Copyright © 1995 by Off the Shelf Publishing, Australia
All rights reserved.

The patterns contained in this book and any items that may be
created from such patterns are intended only for the personal use
and enjoyment of our readers or for presents to be crafted by our
readers. No pattern, or any part or adaptation of any pattern, may
be reproduced, manufactured, or made up for resale or for any
other commercial purpose, including but not limited to the sale of
items at bazaars, swap meets, and crafts fairs, without the express
written consent of the publishers and/or the appropriate license-
holder/s.

First published in the United States 1996
by Dutton Children's Books,
a division of Penguin Books USA Inc.
375 Hudson Street, New York, New York 10014
Originally published in Australia and New Zealand 1995
by Hodder Headline Australia Pty Limited.

Library of Congress Cataloging-in-Publication Data
Souter, Gillian.
Storybook favorites in cross-stitch/Gillian Souter.
— 1st American ed. p. cm.
Includes index.
ISBN 0-525-45613-9 (hardcover)
1. Cross-stitch—Patterns. 2. Children's stories in art.
3. Children's stories—Illustrations. I. Title.
TT778.C76S63 1996
746.44'3—dc20   95-45879
CIP

Photography by Andre Martin
Printed in China
First American Edition
1 3 5 7 9 10 8 6 4 2

AUG 3 1 1998

CONTENTS

INTRODUCTION

This book is filled with ideas—some simple and some more elaborate—for children's gifts in cross-stitch. So that you're not the only one who gets enjoyment out of the process, all the designs are based on favorite characters from children's books. Some of them—Peter Rabbit, Paddington, Winnie-the-Pooh— were my companions as I grew up. Others, such as Spot, Duck, and Angelina, are ones I've grown fond of in my second childhood. Styles of illustration differ greatly, and this is reflected in the designs. Beatrix Potter's delicate watercolors need to be rendered in pastel shades and an impressionistic style. Stitching Dick Bruna's boldly drawn characters is more like coloring in, although you don't see the final effect until the backstitching is added. As the aim was to represent the original illustrations as faithfully as possible, most of the designs are stitched on white backgrounds and use quite a lot of half-stitch (or three-quarter stitch, as it is sometimes called). For those who are new to cross-stitch, the Apple Tree Farm letters, which contain no half-stitches, are a good starting point. Each design is made into a finished project; these are merely suggestions, and there are countless ways of showcasing each design.

BASIC TECHNIQUES

Cross-stitch is one of the most popular of crafts and is extremely simple to learn. If you are new to this form of embroidery, this chapter will give you all the information you need to complete the projects in this book.

In cross-stitch, a pattern is transferred from a charted design to a piece of unmarked fabric. The chart is a grid of squares with symbols forming the design. A key tells you which color of embroidery thread relates to which symbol on the chart. Working the design is simply a matter of stitching a series of crosses in the appropriate color according to the arrangement on the chart.

Types of Fabric

The fabric used for cross-stitch must be of an even weave, that is, have the same number of threads over a given distance both vertically and horizontally. Many types of fabric are suitable for cross-stitch, but either embroidery linen or Aida is ideal. Linen is woven in single threads; Aida has even bands or groups of threads.

The size of each stitch is determined by the number of fabric threads over which you sew and by the number of bands or threads per inch of fabric (known as the fabric count). Most fabric counts are still given in inches, even in countries that have adopted the metric system. Linen 26 has twenty-six threads per inch of fabric, and each stitch

covers two threads (to prevent the embroidery thread gliding under a fabric thread), so there are thirteen stitches per inch. With Linen 30, there are fifteen stitches per inch: the larger the fabric count, the smaller the stitches will be.

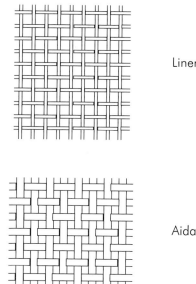

Linen

Aida

Estimating Size

The instructions for each project specify the type of fabric used to stitch it and the amount of fabric required. When you choose a fabric with a different thread count, you will need to calculate what the size of the stitched design will be. Use the following rule: finished size equals the design stitch count divided by the fabric thread count.

When using linen, you stitch over two threads. Therefore, a stitch count of 50 x 50 (i.e., 50 squares on the chart each way) must be divided by 13, if using Linen 26, or by 15 (Linen 30), and so on. Aida also comes in various counts: if using Aida 14, divide the stitch count by 14.

Preparing the Fabric

To prevent the fabric from fraying, zigzag the edges on a sewing machine or simply use masking tape, which can later be removed.

Locate the center of the fabric by folding it in half and then in half again. If you are working on a large design, mark the center with a pin and use a colored thread to tack from side to side and from top to bottom, each time tacking through the center mark. This should quarter your fabric. When you start cross-stitching, make sure the center of the design (indicated by arrows on the chart) matches the center point of your fabric.

Embroidery Thread

Cross-stitch is generally worked in stranded cotton embroidery thread. The designs in this book have all been stitched using DMC stranded cotton. If you wish to use a different brand, match the colors shown in the pictures as closely as possible or choose your own combinations.

The key for each design lists: a symbol that appears in the chart, a corresponding DMC thread number, a color name for easy identification, and the number of stitches to be made in that color. It is impossible to gauge the exact amount of thread needed,

but this will give an idea of the relative quantities required for each color. As a very rough guide, a block of 100 cross-stitches on Aida 14 requires 20" of embroidery thread, using two strands at a time.

The six strands of the embroidery thread can be split into single strands, three lengths of double strands, or other combinations. The number of strands used depends on the count of your fabric. In general, using more strands will make your finished work more vivid, but if you use too many strands they will not fit neatly within the weave of the fabric. Below is a suggested number of strands for different fabric counts. It is a good idea, though, to add an extra strand when stitching the design on a dark fabric.

Count	Cross-stitch strands	Backstitch strands
Aida 11	3	2
Aida 14	2	1
Aida 18	2	1
Aida 22	1	1
Linen 16	3	2
Linen 20	2	1
Linen 26	2	1
Linen 32	1	1

Equipment

Use a blunt needle, such as a small tapestry needle, that will not split the fabric threads. Match the size of the needle to the size of the hole: a size 24 needle is suitable for Linen 20 or Aida 11, whereas a size 26 needle would be appropriate for Aida 14.

You will need two pairs of scissors: a small pair for trimming threads and a pair of shears for cutting the fabric.

If you are stitching one of the larger designs, or any that require several similar shades of embroidery thread, your spare strands can easily become jumbled. To make a simple thread holder like the one pictured, cut a length of sturdy card and use a hole punch to cut holes at regular intervals. Mark the color number and the appropriate symbol alongside the hole and tie your threads as shown.

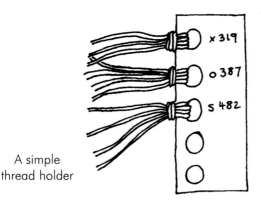

A simple thread holder

A frame or embroidery hoop will help you to stitch evenly and prevent warping, but it is not necessary for very small designs. Choose a hoop that will fit the whole design; otherwise it will damage existing stitches.

Reading the Charts

Each square on the chart represents a full cross-stitch, and each symbol represents a color as specified in the key. A heavy line indicates where to backstitch, and the key will tell you which color to use for each section of backstitching. Arrows indicate the center of the design.

Check the instructions regarding the position of the stitching on the fabric; if there are no specific instructions, orient the fabric to match the chart and stitch the

design in the center. Find the color represented by the center symbol and start on that block of color.

Cut a 20" length of embroidery thread and gently split it into the appropriate number of strands. Let the strands dangle and untwist.

Cross-stitching

Thread the needle with the appropriate number of strands and bring it through the fabric, leaving ¾" of waste thread at the back. Hold this tail carefully and make sure that your first four or five stitches secure it. Then trim any excess.

Stitch a series of diagonal bars running from left to right. Then, at the end of the row, return by stitching the top bars from right to left. Drop your needle to the bottom of the next row and repeat the process. Stitches in a sequence interlock, sharing holes with the neighboring stitch.

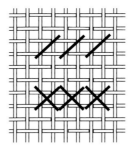

Forming cross-stitches on linen

Forming cross-stitches on Aida

Remember, the number of threads crossed by a single stitch will depend on your fabric: on linen, each stitch covers two threads; on Aida, each stitch covers one band of threads. This is shown more clearly in the two diagrams on page 10.

Always work horizontally rather than vertically and do not change directions; even though you may use more embroidery thread, the result will look much neater.

Once you have stitched some crosses, use them as your reference point and count from them, rather than from the center. Your tacked center lines remain useful as a cross-check that you are counting correctly. Complete each block of color, jumping short distances where necessary, but always securing the thread at the back by running the needle under existing threads. If blocks are some distance apart, finish off the first and start afresh.

To finish off each section, run your needle through the back of four or five stitches and trim the embroidery thread close to the cloth.

Half-stitch

Many of the charts contain some half-stitches, or, as they are sometimes called, three-quarter stitches. These are indicated on the chart by a right-angled triangle and are usually found around the edges of a design. In this case, one diagonal of the cross-stitch is formed in the usual way, but the second stitch is brought down into the central hole of linen, or into the center of an Aida block.

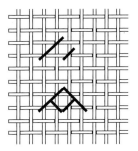

Forming two half-stitches

Where the chart indicates two half-stitches in the same square, you will need to decide which color should predominate in the second diagonal.

Backstitch

Many of the charts include backstitching to define outlines and provide detail. It is indicated by a solid line on the chart. Backstitch is always worked after cross-stitching is completed and is worked in a continuous line. The method is best described in the diagram below.

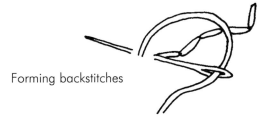

Forming backstitches

Some Tips

It is important to keep your work as clean and fresh as possible. Don't leave unfinished work in an embroidery hoop for too long, as the hoop may mark the fabric. When not in use, always secure the needle at the edge of the fabric to prevent rust marks or thread distortion from spoiling your stitching.

Do not fold work-in-progress; roll it in a layer of tissue paper. A sheet of acetate (available from art supply shops) offers good protection for a large project.

Cut your embroidery thread, as you need it, into 20" lengths. Longer strands will start to fray toward the end.

After working a series of stitches, your thread will start to twist. This can give uneven stitches, so occasionally let the needle dangle down from the fabric so that the thread can unwind.

When moving from one area of a color to another patch of the same color, don't jump the thread across the back if the gap will remain bare. Such leaps will show through the fabric in the finished work.

If you make an error in counting, do not try to rescue the embroidery thread for reuse. Use a pair of small pointed scissors to snip misplaced stitches and carefully pull out the strands, then stitch correctly with a new piece of embroidery thread.

Avoid the temptation to start or finish off with a knot; it will form a lump when the work is laid flat.

Teaching Children

There was a time when every child, or at least every girl, was expected to cross-stitch a sampler. As it was usually a prescribed design of letters and numbers with little or no decoration, it must have seemed more of a chore than a pleasure.

The designs in this book will no doubt tempt many boys and girls to take up the craft of cross-stitch, and it is important to start them on simple and achievable projects that will not dampen their enthusiasm and deter their interest.

Here are some tips:

- Encourage children to practice the basic cross-stitch by creating colored patterns on scrap fabric before tackling a design.

- Explain how the key works, making sure they understand that each symbol represents a particular color.

- Children may like to color in the key and the chart (you may photocopy a design from the book provided it is for personal use only).

- Choose a large-count Aida fabric and a large blunt needle for them to work with.

- Choose a small design that has big blocks of solid color. Introduce half-stitches only once they have mastered the full cross-stitch. The letter designs for *Apple Tree Farm* have no half-stitches, and one of these may be a good starting point.

- Supervise backstitching to begin with. It may be appropriate for you to work the backstitch for younger children.

- Help children make their stitched design into a finished project that they can use or display.

- Help children to chart their own initials, name, or age, using the alphabet and number charts on pages 124–25. If they stitch their name and age on a design, it both personalizes it and becomes a milestone in a child's life.

In the Nursery

The birth of a baby
is a special event and is worth
marking with a handmade gift.
This section includes an array of
wonderful ideas, many of which
will no doubt become treasured
heirlooms. Peter Rabbit adds a
lovely touch to a nursery deco-
rated in pastels, while Madeline
and Babar will brighten the room.
You can also use other designs
from the book to adorn such useful things as a crib sheet, a quilt,
or a travel bag to hold all those
baby necessities.

MADELINE

The small but fearless figure of Madeline has delighted children and grown-ups since a European immigrant to America first penned her adventures in 1939. Ludwig Bemelmans was inspired while recovering in a French hospital after being knocked from his bicycle during a holiday. On the ceiling above his bed was a crack shaped like a rabbit. In the room across from his was a little girl who proudly showed off her appendicitis scar. Drawing on his mother's stories of life as a convent girl, and on his wife's first name, Bemelmans gave the world Madeline. This first, prizewinning book was eventually followed by another five tales in which Madeline, along with her fellow students and their teacher, Miss Clavel, make friends with a boy named Pepito and a dog called Genevieve, and overcome many challenges—all the while continuing to walk, eat, and sleep in two straight lines.

Sleeping Bag

Whether the new arrival is a boy, a girl, or twins, this roomy pinafore-bag will give everyone sweet dreams.

Materials: 9" x 5" white Aida fabric
with 14 thread groups per inch;
colored fabric; backing fabric;
elastic; press studs;
DMC embroidery threads listed.

Stitch count: 39H x 44W

Directions: Stitch the design. Cut backing fabric to fit the stitched bib and sew them together with right sides facing. Turn the bib inside out. Cut two 23" x 18" pieces of fabric to make the bag and two straps, each 18" x 3". With right sides facing, sew the bag pieces together along the long sides and one short side. On the fourth side, sew a casing to fit your elastic. Thread elastic through the casing and slip stitch the gap closed. Turn the bag right side out.

With right sides facing, sew the bib to the bag, press and top stitch. Fold the straps, right sides together, in half lengthwise and sew along the length and across one end. Turn the straps right side out. Fold in ragged ends and slip stitch. Sew the straps to the back of the bib. Sew press studs on the end of each strap and inside the back of the bag.

	KEY for Madeline & Pepito		
	DMC	Color	Stitches
O	307	yellow	165
■	310	black	42
▼	469	dark olive	201
U	470	olive	118
X	666	red	44
+	754	pink	70
*	919	brown	39
•		white	21
	310	black	backstitch

17

Madeline and Pepito (the son of the Spanish ambassador) make a charming couple on the front of this sleeping bag. See page 17 for instructions.

Two Madelines is a somewhat daunting thought, but both will be welcome additions to a baby's room. The charts for both sizes appear on pp. 20–21.

Welcome Card

A card featuring Madeline in her best pinafore makes a lovely welcome for a little girl.

Materials: 6" x 4" cream Aida fabric with 11 thread groups per inch; colored card; double-sided tape; DMC embroidery threads listed.

Stitch count: 44H x 29W

Directions: Stitch the design on fabric and press. Cut 6" x 12" of card and score it with a knife to create three equal panels. Trim a narrow strip off the left panel. Cut a window in the center panel to fit the design. Stick double-sided tape on the inside of the center panel, position the embroidery, and stick down the left-hand panel as a backing.

KEY for Madeline			
DMC	Color	Petite	Grande
U 307	yellow	118	450
■ 310	black	68	77
X 666	red	14	53
O 754	pink	60	211
— 798	blue	224	874
+ 919	brown	48	164
• white		32	114
310	black		backstitch

Heirloom Doll

Give a newborn baby a Madeline doll, and you can be sure that it will become a friend for the whole of childhood.

Materials: 10" x 6" cream Aida fabric with 11 thread groups per inch; 10" x 6" backing fabric; polyester stuffing; black ribbon; DMC embroidery threads listed.

Stitch count: 90H x 45W

Directions: Stitch the design on the Aida fabric and carefully press the finished work. Trim around the design, allowing a 1" margin, and zigzag to secure edges. Trim and zigzag backing fabric to match. Lay the two together with right sides facing and sew around the design, allowing a ½" seam and leaving a gap between the doll's legs. Turn the doll right side out and fill it with polyester stuffing. Hand-sew the gap closed. Fold a length of black ribbon in half and stitch the fold along the side of the hat.

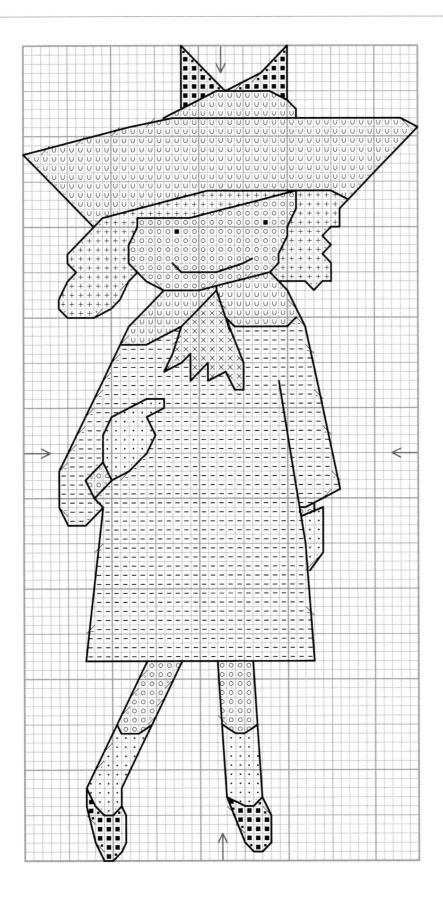

PETER RABBIT

This most famous of rabbits first appeared in an illustrated letter written by Beatrix Potter to cheer up a little boy who was ill in bed. Potter's own childhood had been a rather lonely one, and on September 4, 1893, she wrote, "My dear Noel, I don't know what to write to you, so I shall tell you a story." In the following eight pages, she told the story that was to become the most popular children's book of all time—The Tale of Peter Rabbit. It was some years before Potter could find a publisher for her story, but once it appeared, in 1902, it was a great commercial success, and she went on to create many more books suitable for small hands. The characters, including Jemima Puddle-Duck, Mrs. Tiggy-Winkle, and Benjamin Bunny, were based on real creatures: pets and wildlife found in the Lake District, where Potter spent her holidays and later chose to live. The accuracy of her paintings and the gentle humor in her text ensured the lasting success of Beatrix Potter's books, which have been published in many languages and are still enjoyed by children and parents alike.

Copyright © Frederick Warne & Co., 1995

Birth Announcement

Many of Beatrix Potter's best-loved characters are woven into this beautiful birth announcement. Most of the work can be done while waiting for the baby's arrival.

Materials: 18" x 16" white linen
with 26 threads per inch;
DMC embroidery threads listed.

Stitch count: 180H x 153W

Directions: Tack marking lines to divide the fabric into four (see page 9) and stitch the characters and the backstitching. Use the alphabet and number charts on pages 124–25 to chart the baby's name and date of birth on graph paper. Cross-stitch these in position. Press the completed work carefully and have it professionally framed.

KEY for Beatrix Potter sampler

	DMC	Color	Stitches		DMC	Color	Stitches
X	353	peach	675	−	775	pale blue	218
*	413	charcoal	12	+	794	blue	257
S	414	light gray	68	I	841	fawn	371
I	437	tan	206	\	842	light fawn	99
▼	471	dark green	34	▲	932	gray-blue	121
O	472	green	318	II	976	very dark tan	81
F	504	mint	174	T	977	dark tan	186
U	543	light peach	127	↑	3689	pink	132
●	640	brown	60	L	3713	pale pink	181
4	642	light brown	138	•		white	268
=	644	sand	70				
>	712	cream	164				
N	738	light tan	296				
<	760	rose	146				

Backstitch

310	black	hedgehog
794	blue	tendrils
413	charcoal	other details

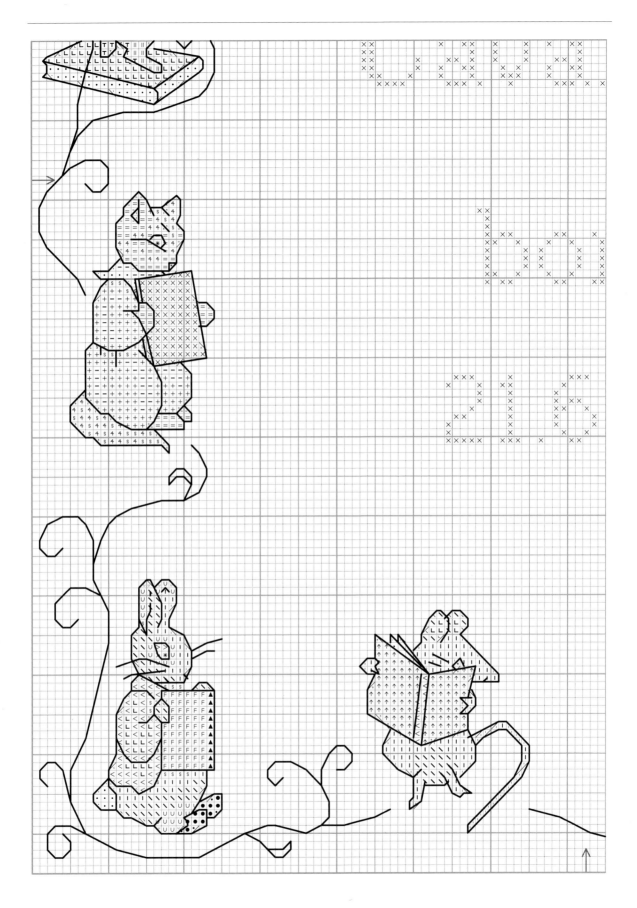

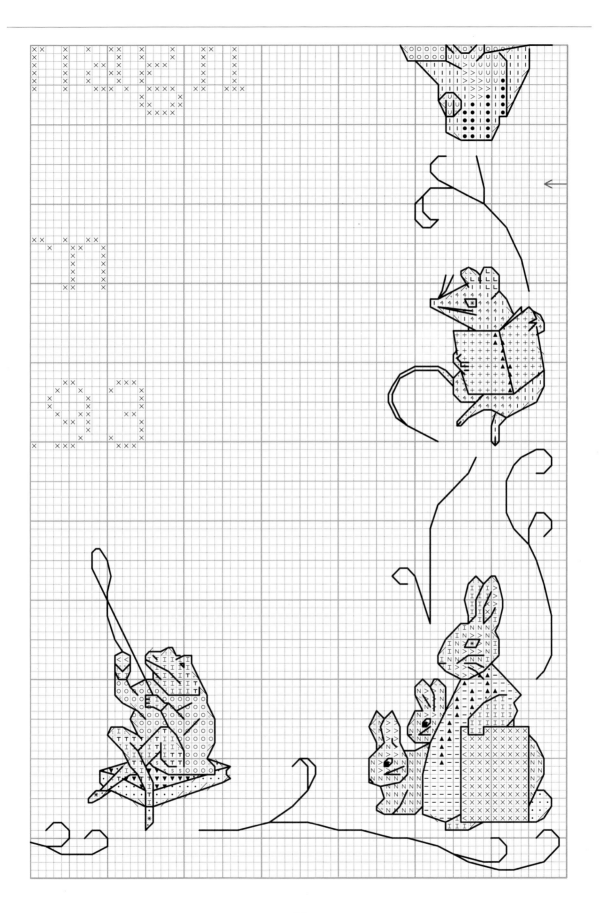

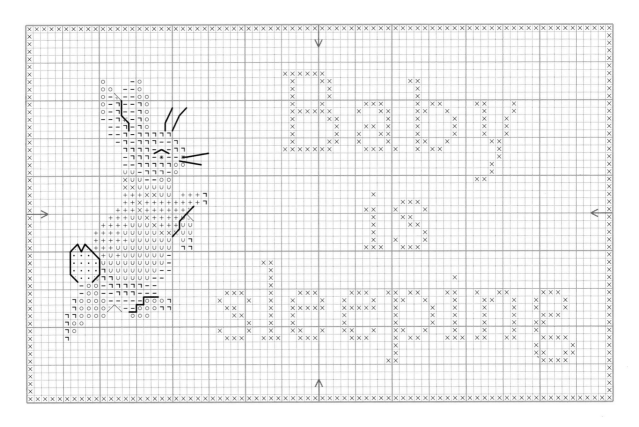

Sleep Notice

Peter Rabbit, in his classic pose, guards the door of a sleeping child. As an option, you could replace "Baby" with a name.

Materials: 12" x 10" white Aida fabric
with 11 thread groups per inch;
16" ribbon;
9" x 6½" felt;
8½" x 6" heavy white card stock;
DMC embroidery threads listed.

Stitch count: 50H x 80W

Directions: Stitch the design, inserting a child's name if desired (see pages 124–25). Carefully press the work. Cut an 8½" x 6" piece of white card. Center the embroidered work over the card, fold the edges over, and glue them onto the back of the card, so that the work is taut. Cut a 16" length of ribbon and glue the ends at the back of the top right and left corners. Cut a 9" x 6½" rectangle of felt and glue it to cover the back of the notice. The felt should extend evenly around all edges as a border.

	KEY for Peter Rabbit		
	DMC	Color	Stitches
✱	413	gray	2
┐	437	dark tan	64
–	738	tan	64
O	739	light tan	48
×	798	dark blue	535
U	809	blue	71
+	3747	pale blue	54
•		white	18
	413	gray	backstitch

Pin Holder

Mrs. Tiggy-Winkle, the hedgehog who takes in the animals' washing, seems an ideal decoration for this safety-pin holder.

Materials: 8" x 8" white linen
with 26 threads per inch;
8" x 8" colored fabric;
polyester toy stuffing;
DMC embroidery threads listed.

Stitch count: 52H x 52W

Directions: Stitch the design in the center of the fabric and carefully press the finished work. Zigzag the edges of both the linen and the backing fabric. Place the two pieces together with right sides facing and sew them together, leaving a 1" gap along one edge. Turn the pillow inside out so that the design faces out and fill it with the polyester stuffing. Neatly hand-sew the opening closed. Attach safety pins for a useful gift.

	KEY for Mrs. Tiggy-Winkle		
	DMC	Color	Stitches
■	310	black	3
Z	318	light gray	89
X	434	brown	248
>	436	light brown	267
U	472	green	115
●	601	dark pink	30
−	603	pink	54
O	605	light pink	80
\	793	blue	115
▲	801	dark brown	95
↑	3747	light blue	85
+		ecru	52
=		white	308

Backstitch

	310	black	face, cloth
	801	dark brown	spines
	317	dark gray	other

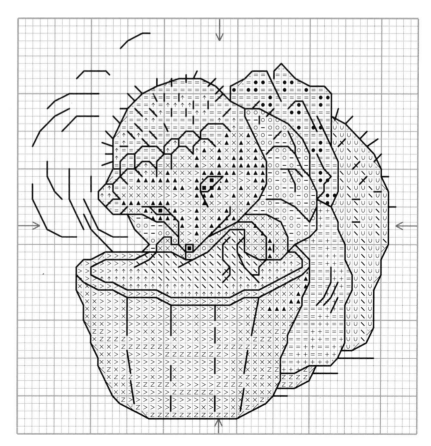

Right: This cushion for safely holding diaper pins features Mrs. Tiggy-Winkle; see page 29. Instructions for the lidded box can be found on page 32.

Below: Peter Rabbit offers a gentle warning not to disturb. The pattern appears on page 28, along with instructions for making the sign.

Lidded Box

This fabric-covered box is ideal for holding cotton balls or diaper pins. The lid features Mrs. Rabbit dosing a slightly ill but very naughty Peter with camomile tea.

Materials: 6" x 6" white Aida fabric
                 with 14 thread groups per inch;
                 thin batting;
                 heavy card stock;
                 colored fabric;
                 DMC embroidery threads listed.

Stitch count: 56H x 56W

Directions: Stitch the design on the Aida fabric and press the finished work. Trim this into a circle, allowing ½" around the stitched border.

Cut a strip 1½" wide and 16" long on the diagonal of the colored fabric, creating a bias strip. Position the strip face down on the stitched design and sew the edges, allowing a ¼" seam. Zigzag edges to secure.

Use a compass to draw five circles on card: one with a 2½" radius, two with a 2¼" radius, and two with a 2" radius. Cut out each disk and attach a layer of batting to the largest one with dabs of glue. Place the Aida over the wadding and glue the raw edge of the bias strip on the back of the card.

Cover one of the 2¼" radius disks as a base. Cut a piece of card 16" x 2½" and glue the short ends to form a cylinder to fit the covered base. Cut a 16½" x 3¼" strip of fabric and glue it around the cylinder. Snip darts in the fabric overlapping the base and glue them down. Cut a 14" x 2" piece of card and cover one side with fabric, gluing down each edge at the back. Glue this piece around the inside of the box, as a lining.

Cover the two smaller disks and glue one onto the underneath of the lid and the other inside the box. Cover the last disk and glue it onto the outside base of the box, covering the tabs.

KEY for Mrs. Rabbit & Peter			
	DMC	Color	Stitches
X	353	apricot	185
T	414	gray	2
Z	437	tan	25
∩	738	light tan	62
+	739	cream	186
U	772	pale green	102
▲	813	blue	83
/	818	pink	161
O	827	pale blue	127
*	928	ice	55
N	954	green	31
•		white	448
	414	gray	backstitch

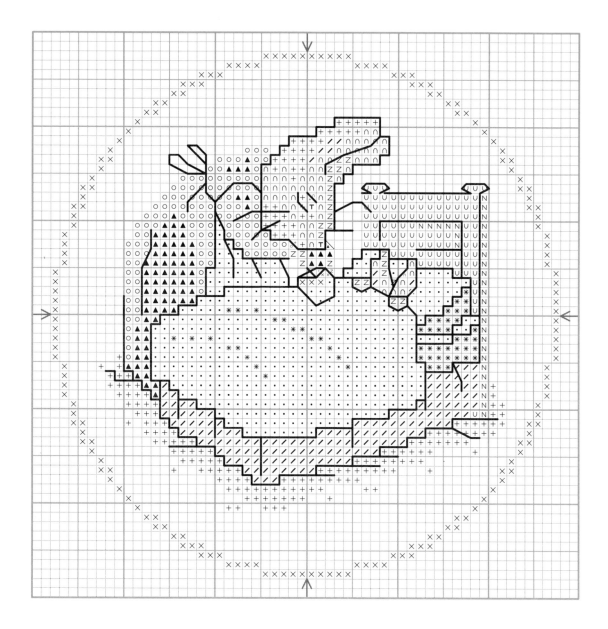

♕ BABAR ♕

Over sixty years ago, a Parisian mother made up a lively bedtime story about a young elephant who grows up to become a wise and much-loved king. Cécile de Brunhoff's sons were so enchanted by the tale that they recounted it to their artist father, Jean, and persuaded him to illustrate it. The adventures of Babar, who was given a dashing green jacket and a red bow tie, were produced in book form through the good grace of two uncles in the publishing industry, and a classic of children's literature was born. Jean de Brunhoff wrote and illustrated another eleven Babar books before his death from tuberculosis. After such a family effort, it was a natural conclusion that Laurent, the eldest of those children to hear the bedtime story, should continue the tradition. The many books have since been translated from French into twelve languages, and an animated version is winning Babar new friends around the world.

Babar characters ™ & © 1994 Laurent de Brunhoff.
All rights reserved.

Soft Toys

Bright, solid colors soon catch a baby's eye, and these delightful Babar and Celeste toys will make great crib companions.

Materials: 10" x 8" white Aida fabric
with 11 thread groups per inch;
10" x 8" backing fabric;
polyester toy stuffing;
DMC embroidery threads listed.

Stitch count: 62H x 51W — Babar
63H x 41W — Celeste

Directions: Stitch the design on the Aida fabric and carefully press the finished work. Trim around the design, allowing a ¾" margin, and zigzag to secure edges. Trim and zigzag backing fabric to match. Lay the two together with right sides facing and sew around the design, allowing a ¼" seam, and leaving a 1" gap.

Turn the toy right side out and fill it with polyester stuffing. Hand-sew the gap closed, making sure no stuffing can be pulled out.

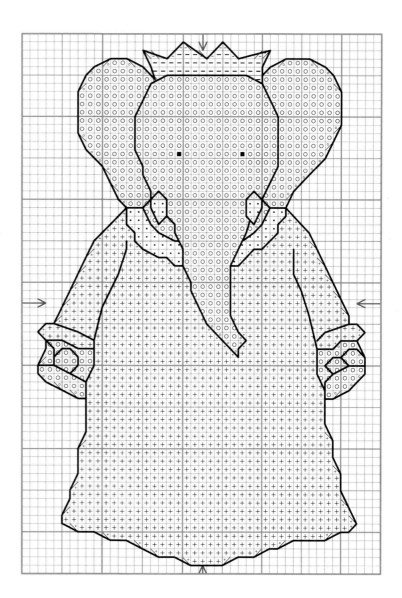

	DMC	Color	Stitches
■	310	black	51
✱	350	rose	8
○	453	gray	1288
✕	702	green	1178
+	892	pink	1159
−	972	yellow	99
•		white	120
	310	black	backstitch

KEY for Babar and Celeste

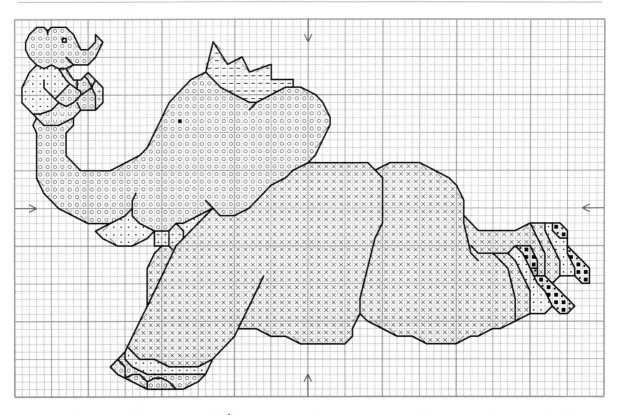

Bath Wrap

Keep baby snug after a bath with this elegant bath wrap. The hood features Babar and one of his triplets.

Materials: 16" x 9" white Aida fabric with 14 thread groups per inch; 48" x 35" white terry cloth; 5½ yards white bias binding; DMC embroidery threads listed.

Stitch count: 48H x 77W

Directions: Stitch the design in the center of the Aida. Cut a 35" square of terry cloth and position the stitched design across one corner. Trim the short edges of the Aida to form a right-angled triangle. Cut an extra piece of terry cloth to match this. Round all corners and zigzag all edges.

Sew the two triangles together with the design on top and bind the long edge with bias binding. Position this triangle on a corner of the terry cloth square, with the design face up, and sew along the two short edges. Finish the edges of the square with a length of bias binding.

Right: Height chart instructions are on page 40.

™ & © 1994 L. de Brunhoff. All rights reserved.

	DMC	Color	Stitches
■	310	black	34
+	350	rose	18
O	453	gray	556
X	702	green	1025
U	793	blue	14
–	972	yellow	44
•		white	108
	310	black	backstitch

KEY for Babar & baby

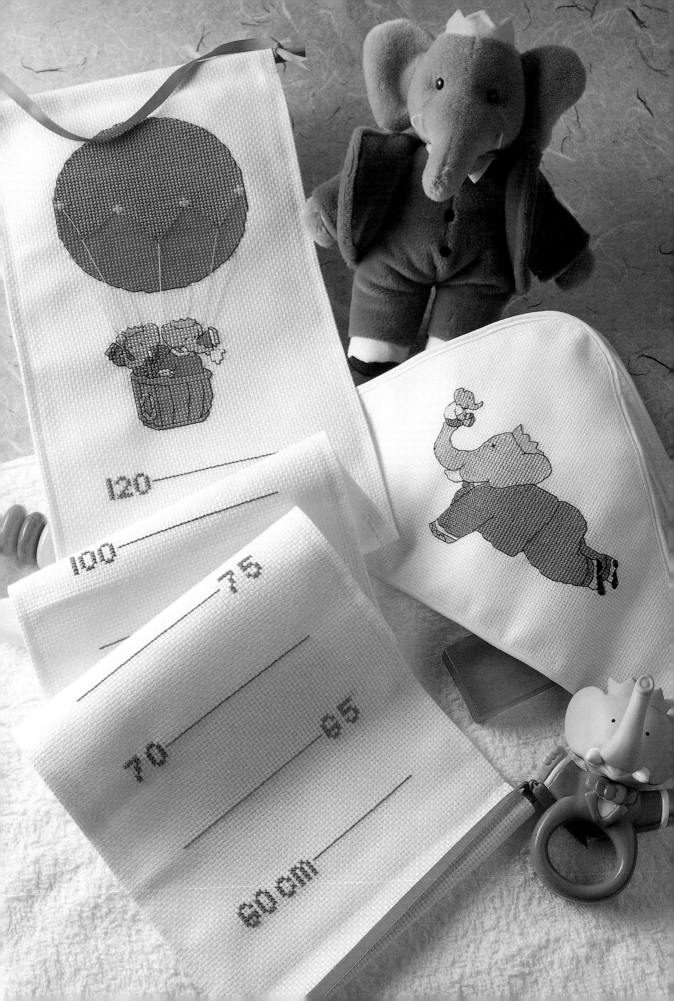

Height Chart

A height chart is an essential item in every child's room. Pin strips of ribbon as markers that can be moved up the chart over time.

Materials: 38" x 9" white Aida fabric
with 11 thread groups per inch;
38" x 9" white fabric;
green ribbon;
thin dowel;
metallic gold thread;
DMC embroidery threads listed.

Stitch count: 103H x 54W

Directions: Stitch the design at the top of the Aida fabric, allowing 3" above the balloon for the casing. Note that the dash lines are long stitches of gold thread. One and one-half inches below the design, cross-stitch "4 ft" on the left-hand side and backstitch a line across the chart (see pages 124–25). (Please note that the photograph shows the height designations in centimeters. Use the chart on page 126 as a guide for "ft." and "in." design.) Two inches below, on the right-hand side, cross-stitch "10 in." Add a backstitch line. Continue on down the chart, stitching the number of inches two inches below the previous one on the right-hand side. Stitch "3 ft" on the left-hand side below the line marking "2 in" and repeat the sequence. Then stitch "2 ft" on the left-hand side. (The chart is hung above floor level.)

Zigzag the edges of the Aida fabric and carefully press the work. Back the Aida with the white fabric, turn over ½" along the long sides of the Aida, press, and sew ¼" from the edge. Fold the top edge over 1¼" and sew across 1" from the fold to create a casing for the dowel. Repeat at the base.

KEY for Babar's balloon			
	DMC	Color	Stitches
✳	350	rose	884
O	453	gray	191
+	702	green	1488
✕	892	pink	81
–	972	yellow	74
U	976	tan	280
•		white	38
Backstitch			
	310	black	solid lines
	972	gold	dash lines

Cut two 10" lengths of dowel and insert in the top and bottom casings. Cut a 16" piece of ribbon and tie each end to the ends of the top dowel, forming a hanging loop. Cut a piece of ribbon 12" in length and tie each end to the ends of the bottom dowel, securing it in place.

Babar characters ™ & © 1994 L. de Brunhoff.
All rights reserved.

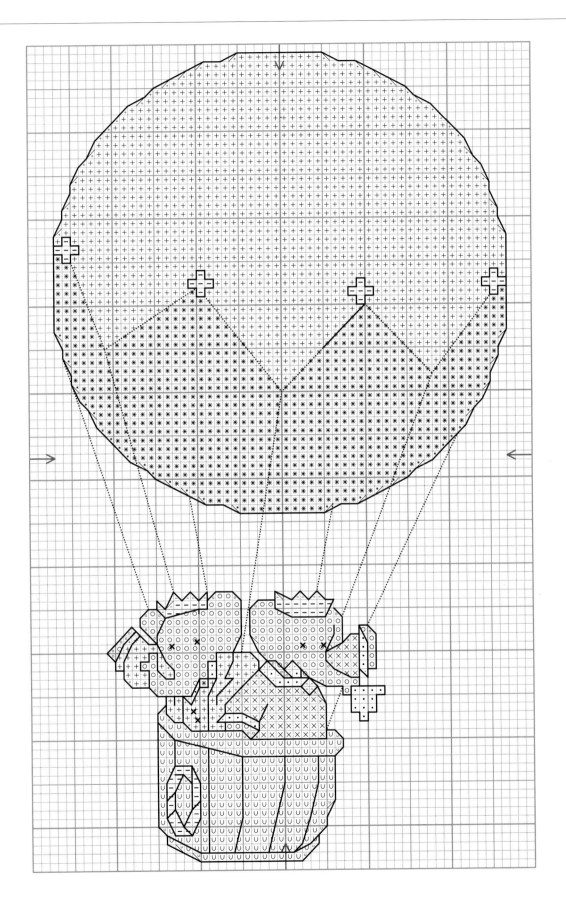

For Toddlers

These early years
are a time of pure delight as
youngsters try their first steps,
learn their first words, and begin
to discover the joy of books. Here
are many characters who will
become fast friends: Spot, Miffy,
Paddington, and the endearing
Duck, all used to decorate toys
and objects suitable for this age
group. Personalized gifts will become prized possessions with those
toddlers who have just learned
that useful word "Mine!"

SPOT

The lovable puppy known as Spot first appeared on bookshelves in Eric Hill's award-winning Where's Spot?, which was published in 1980. Within weeks, the delightful lift-the-flap book was at the top of the best-seller list, leading to a whole series of stories about Spot. Eric Hill was a graphic designer and illustrator when he created the first Spot book to amuse his young son. The bright colors, gentle humor and intriguing design are a winning combination. Spot, whose favorite activities are hiding, exploring, and opening presents, makes a wonderful introduction to the world of books. His adventures have been translated into over sixty languages, including Arabic, Manx, and Urdu, and there are many dual-language editions, such as English-Braille. All in all, over twenty million copies have been sold. Spot is a multimedia star, appearing in his own animated series.

KEY for Spot eating			
	DMC	Color	Stitches
O	307	yellow	493
■	310	black	51
✳	433	dark brown	71
+	725	gold	615
U	754	light peach	6
✕	976	tan	65
	310	black	backstitch

Copyright © Eric Hill/Salspot, 1995

Feeding Bib

Delight a special child with this image from Where's Spot?, one of the best-selling children's books ever published.

Materials: 10" x 12" white Aida fabric with 14 thread groups per inch; 10" x 12" white fabric; 2¼ yards of red bias binding; DMC embroidery threads listed.

Stitch count: 35H x 58W

Directions: Stitch the design in the lower half of the Aida fabric. On a large piece of paper, draw the 9" x 11" bib shape, using the pattern on page 126 as a guide. Make sure the neck hole is large enough to fit the baby comfortably.

Pin the paper pattern onto the fabric and the backing, making sure that your design is in the correct position. Cut both fabrics in the bib shape. Remove the pattern and zigzag the fabric edges together.

Trim the outside edges with bias binding. Pin a 40" strip of bias binding around the neckline so that the ties are of even length. Starting at one tie end, sew the bias binding edges together; continue sewing around the neckline and up to the end of the other tie.

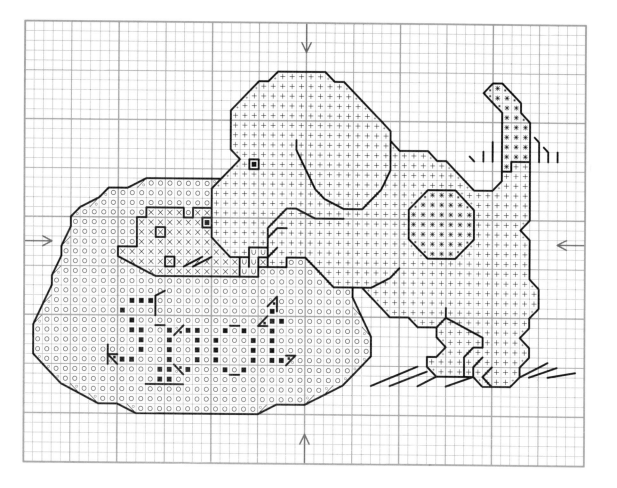

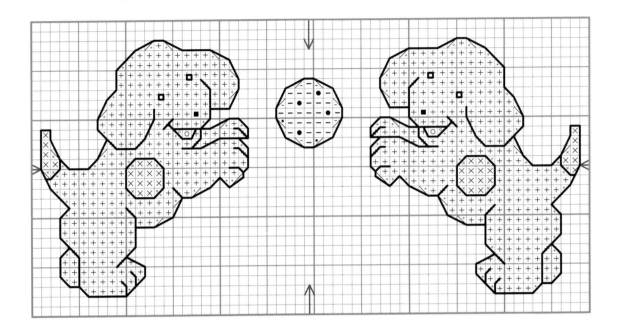

Towel Trim

This simple design of Spot at play is quick and easy to stitch. To adapt the motif for a longer trim, omit the mirrored figure and repeat the remaining design.

Materials: A hand towel;
a strip of white Aida fabric
(or a towel with an Aida inset);
DMC embroidery threads listed.

Stitch count: 26H x 60W (adaptable)

Directions: Check the width of the towel and stitch the design so that the figures are evenly spaced. If making a band to apply to a towel, cut a strip of Aida fabric 1" wider than the width of the towel and stitch the design along the center. Fold the raw edges to the back and press flat. Baste the strip onto your towel and then slip-stitch along the edges, turning the ends in neatly. Press the towel carefully to complete.

KEY for Spot and ball			
	DMC	Color	Stitches
■	310	black	2
×	433	dark brown	48
●	444	yellow	6
−	666	red	31
+	725	gold	610
○	754	light peach	4
	310	black	backstitch

Right: A hand towel and feeding bib make a delightful set. Instructions for the bib can be found on page 45.

Spot ™ © Ventura Ltd 1995. Licensed by Copyrights

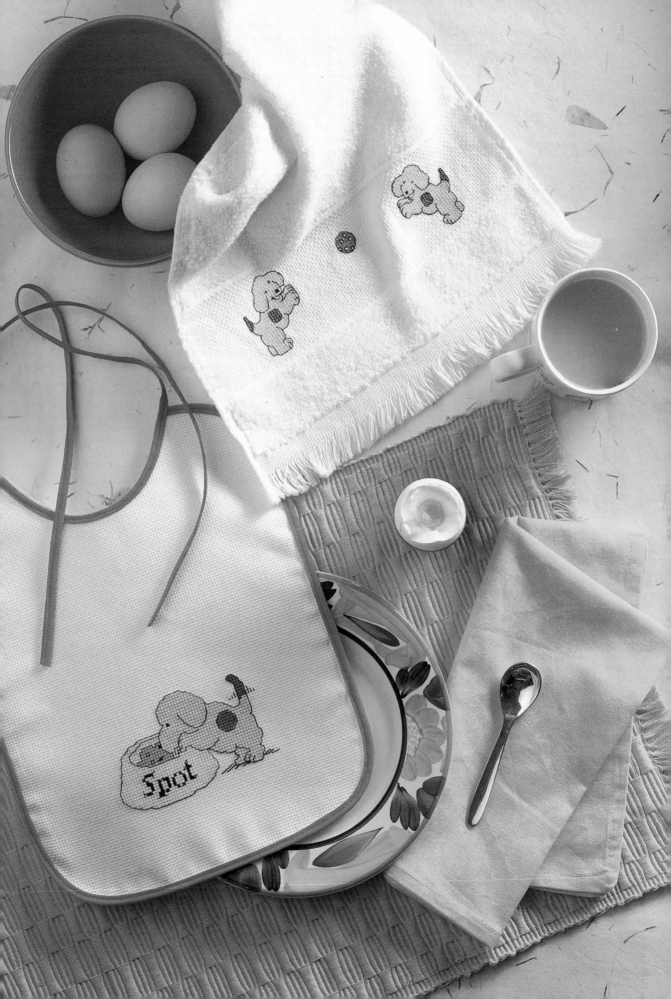

Artwork Folder

This colorful folder is ideal for storing a child's works of art. A photograph of the finished project can be found on page 51.

Materials: 8" x 10" white Aida fabric
with 14 thread groups per inch;
13½" x 20" heavy white cardboard;
14" x 20½" red cardboard;
double-sided tape;
bookbinding tape;
DMC embroidery threads listed;
extra thread for cords.

Stitch count: 61H x 86W

	DMC	Color	Stitches
■	310	black	11
‖	350	rose	90
✕	433	dark brown	101
●	444	yellow	3
U	703	green	67
+	725	gold	1145
Z	754	light peach	6
O	798	blue	138
✳	918	rust	86
•	922	tan	879
▲	996	light blue	97
	310	black	backstitch

KEY for Spot painting

48

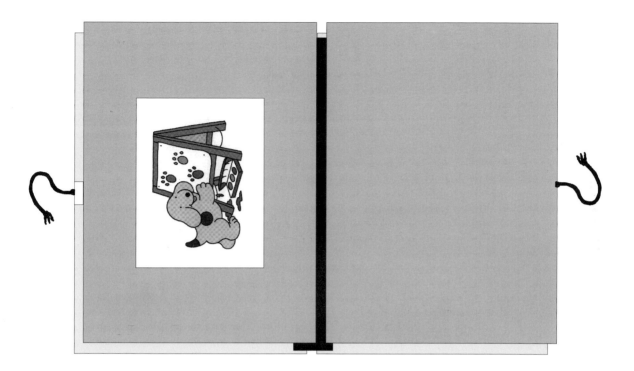

Directions: Stitch the design in the
center of the Aida fabric and press flat. Cut
the white card into two pieces, each 13½" x
10". Lay one on top of the other and use
bookbinding tape to tape them together
along one long edge. Position double-sided
tape on one side of the folder and stick down
the stitched design so that it is centered.

Cut three lengths of embroidery thread,
each 20", braid them, and tie a knot ½" up
from each end. Cut the braid in half and
knot the ends; you should have two cords.
Tape one cord in the center of the top edge
of both the front and the back card.

Cut the red card into two pieces, each
one 14" x 10¼" in size. Cut a window, 7" x
5½", in one piece of card to frame the cross-
stitch. Stick double-sided tape at the edges
of the white card and around the window on
the red card. Position the red card over the
design and stick it down. Cover the back
with the second sheet of red card. Trim the
edges of the red card to fit the white cards.
Tie the cords to complete.

Diagram of Artwork Folder
showing the boards, binding
tape, cords, cross-stitch, and
covering card.

Right: An attractive folder is ideal for safekeeping the best pictures created by a child. The chart and instructions for making this can be found on pages 48–49.

Below: This sturdy bag will hold plenty of special picture books. Instructions are on page 52.

Book Bag

Every child needs a bag in which to carry his or her Spot books. This one will also fit larger picture books and is ideal for trips to the library. It is pictured on page 50.

Materials: 10" x 12" white Aida fabric
with 14 thread groups per inch;
10" x 12" of white fabric;
40" x 20" colored fabric;
colored bias binding;
DMC embroidery threads listed.

Stitch count: 70H x 67W

Directions: Stitch the design on the Aida fabric so that the 12" edges form the top and bottom. Carefully press the finished stitching.

Cut the Aida into a flap, 10½" wide and 8½" high, with the design 1" from the bottom edge. Round off the bottom two corners and cut a matching piece of white fabric as backing. Zigzag the edges of both layers to prevent fraying and sew colored bias binding around the sides and base.

Cut a piece of colored fabric measuring 27" x 12" to make the body of the bag. Zigzag all edges. Sew a 1½" hem along one short edge. Align the other short edge with the untrimmed edge of the flap section and sew the Aida and colored fabric together, with right sides facing. Press the seam and hand-sew the edge of the white backing fabric down to cover it.

Cut two 12½" x 2" strips of colored fabric to form the sides of the bag. Zigzag all edges and sew a ½" hem at one short edge of each strip. Lay a strip along one edge of the body section so that the hemmed end is aligned with the start of the Aida flap. Sew the side strip onto the body section, with right sides facing. Repeat on the other side.

To make the handle, cut a strip of colored fabric, 30" x 3", and zigzag the raw edges. Fold the piece in half lengthwise and sew a ½" seam to form a long fabric tube. Turn the tube inside out and press flat. Hand-sew each end inside the bag sides, allowing a 1" overlap for strength.

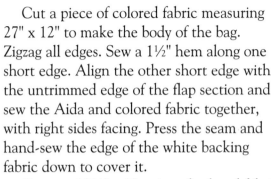

	KEY for Spot reading		
	DMC	Color	Stitches
∗	310	black	5
•	350	rose	351
✕	433	brown	95
U	444	yellow	47
O	721	orange	431
+	725	gold	1312
<	905	green	120
▲	3765	blue	41
	310	black	backstitch

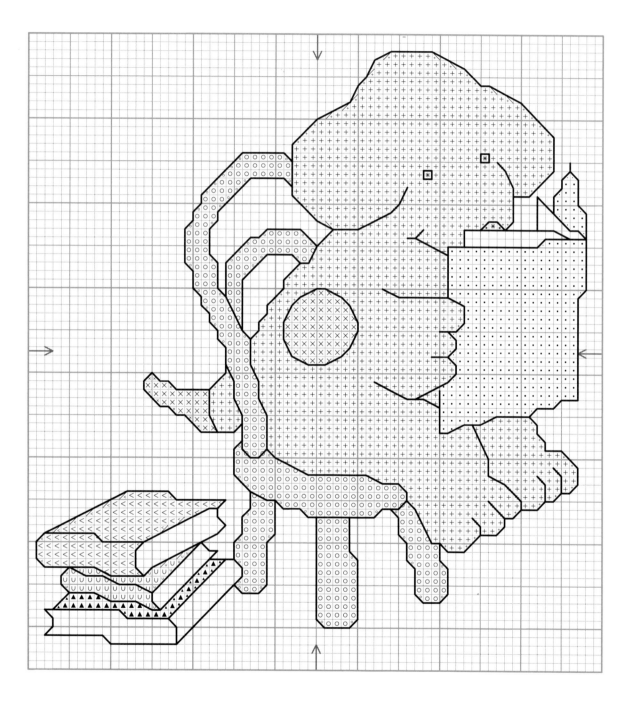

Miffy

Kitty

MIFFY

The simple lines and bright colors that distinguish Miffy and her friends from other characters are the trademark of Dick Bruna, a remarkably innovative artist and author. Bruna was born in Utrecht, in the Netherlands, in 1927, and even as a small child he enjoyed drawing. His first book was published in 1953, and it introduced a new concept in books for the young, designed as it was for the child, rather than for the parent. Bruna created Miffy, one of his most popular characters, after watching his own children play with a pet rabbit. His use of bold, contrasting colors has since been adopted by other illustrators, but none have achieved the same worldwide success. Dick Bruna's books, which include a whole series of Miffy adventures, have been translated into many languages from the original Dutch and have recently been animated for television. Miffy, Pussy Nell, and Snuffy are today as enchanting to his young audience as they were forty years ago.

Illustrations Dick Bruna, © copyright Mercis b.v., 1970

Napkin Ring 🌸 🌼

Pussy Nell is featured here on a napkin ring. She could also be used on other party items, such as crackers, name tags, and place mats.

Materials: 8" x 4" white Aida fabric
with 14 thread groups per inch;
2" wide white Aida band;
a cardboard or plastic tube;
double-sided tape;
DMC embroidery threads listed.

Stitch count: 22H x 16W

Directions: Stitch the design in the center of the Aida fabric, with short edges at the top and bottom. Zigzag the edges to prevent fraying. Find a cardboard tube large enough to hold a napkin and cut a section 2" wide. Wind double-sided tape around the outside of the tube and cover it with the Aida fabric. Hand-sew the overlapping end. Fold the edges inside the tube and hand-sew the two edges with a lacing stitch. Cut a piece of Aida band to fit inside the tube and hand-sew it in place.

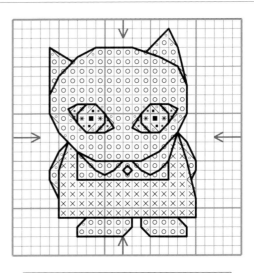

	KEY for Miffy and Pussy Nell		
	DMC	Color	Stitches
■	310	black	6
+	444	yellow	94
✳	701	green	20
✕	797	blue	98
○		white	410
	310	black	backstitch

Gift Sack 🌸 🌼 🌺

There are a thousand uses for this bright little sack, which takes only a few minutes to make up once Miffy has been stitched.

Materials: 12" x 5" red Aida fabric
with 14 thread groups per inch;
ribbon;
DMC embroidery threads listed.

Stitch count: 26H x 25W

Directions: Fold the fabric in half to form a 6" x 5" rectangle. Stitch the design 1" from the folded base. With the design facing inward, sew the side seams and zigzag all edges to prevent fraying. Turn the bag inside out. Fold over and sew a ½" hem at the opening. Fill the sack with small treats and tie it closed with a ribbon.

Pajamas

Cross-stitching over waste canvas is a great way to decorate plain clothes. Here a cherub from the original Miffy book adorns an inexpensive top.

Materials: 7" x 7" waste canvas
with 6.5 thread groups per inch;
blue fleecy top and pants;
DMC embroidery threads listed.

Stitch count: 52H x 53W

Directions: Position the waste canvas on the front of the top, ensuring that it is squared up. Tack around the edges and diagonally so that the canvas is securely attached. Stitch the design, using three strands of embroidery thread. When stitching is complete, remove tacking thread, dampen canvas with a cloth, and carefully pull out the waste canvas strands.

Alternatively, this design could be stitched on blue Aida fabric.

KEY for cherub			
	DMC	Color	Stitches
×	972	yellow	197
O		white	870
	310	black	backstitch

Above: All children are angels when they're asleep. The pattern for this quick project appears on page 57.

Illustrations Dick Bruna, © copyright Mercis b.v., 1963

Right: A set of finger puppets on a stand will give small children hours of simple fun. Instructions are on page 61.

Illustrations Dick Bruna,
© copyright Mercis b.v., 1974

Finger Puppets

Dick Bruna has a wonderful way of simplifying the adult world. This collection of sailor, clown, town mayor, knight, and farmer make ideal finger puppets for small people, as pictured on page 59.

Materials: 5" x 5" Aida fabric
with 14 thread groups per inch;
white backing fabric;
colored cotton fabric;
DMC embroidery threads listed.

Stitch count: approximately 45H x 25W

Directions: Stitch each design on a piece of Aida fabric. For each puppet, cut two 5" squares of backing fabric and one of colored cotton. Lay the cross-stitching face down on a backing square and sew along the base, ¼" below the bottom row of cross-stitches. Trim the edge and zigzag it, then turn the piece inside out so that the design faces out and is backed with the white fabric. Baste ¼" around the figure, stitching the layers together.

Sew the other backing square and the colored square together along one side, forming the base. Trim the edge and zigzag, then turn the piece inside out.

Place the two sections together with the bases aligned and with the cross-stitching and colored fabric facing each other. Sew them together, using the basted outline as a guide. Trim the edges and zigzag to secure threads. Turn the puppet inside out and use a teaspoon to shape the head.

To make a puppet stand, drill holes in a narrow block of wood and glue in short sections of dowel.

Illustrations Dick Bruna, © copyright Mercis b.v., 1974

KEY for Bruna people			
	DMC	Color	Stitches
■	310	black	653
O	318	gray	581
–	702	green	500
X	798	blue	613
+	946	orange	1020
U	973	yellow	615
<	976	brown	66
•		white	137
	310	black	backstitch

PADDINGTON

There have been many bears in children's stories, but the figure of a small furry bear in a duffle coat and battered hat can only conjure up one name: Paddington. This charming bear with a great fondness for marmalade was found one day in London's Paddington Station by the kindhearted Mr. and Mrs. Brown. Paddington's Aunt Lucy in Peru had taken the precaution of tying a luggage label around his neck that read: "Please look after this BEAR," and so he joined the Brown household at number thirty-two Windsor Gardens. When Michael Bond wrote A Bear Called Paddington in the late 1950's, he created a wonderful character who could turn ordinary activities— having a bath, home decorating, going to the movies—into quite extraordinary happenings. Further adventures kept children vastly amused, and a series of picture books based on the character made Paddington a firm favorite with even the very young. Any bear who keeps a trusty marmalade sandwich under his hat in case of emergencies has to be a little bit special.

PADDINGTON BEAR ™
© Paddington and Company Ltd 1995
Licensed by Copyrights

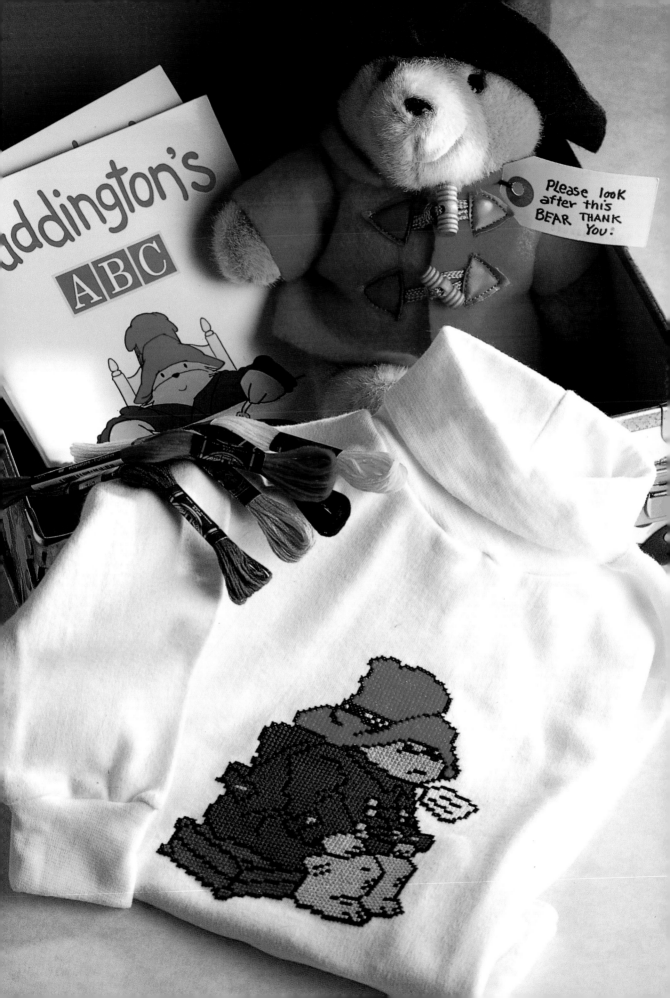

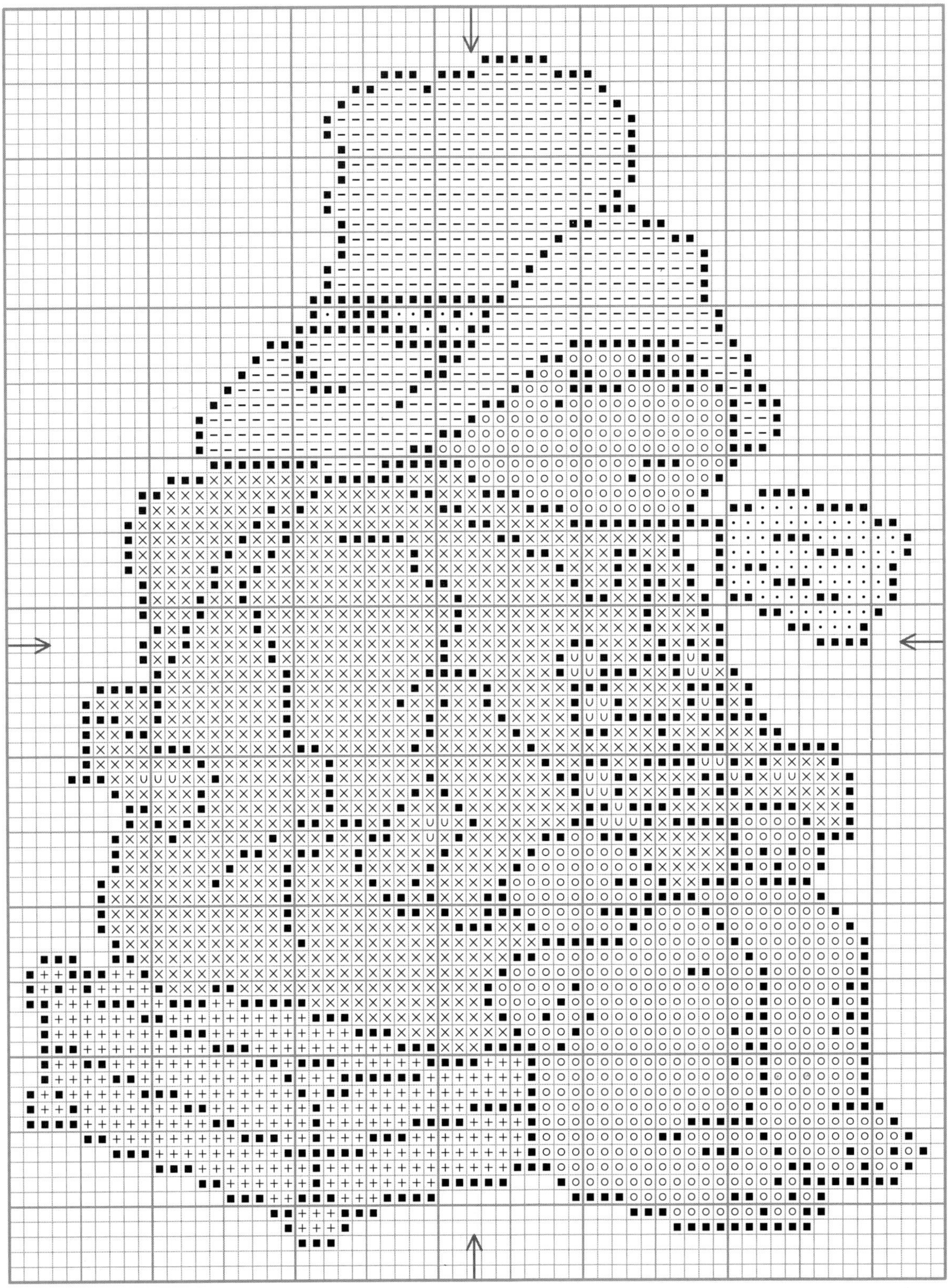

Child's Top

The quintessential image of Paddington is this one: newly arrived from darkest Peru and sitting on his suitcase. In place of back-stitching, this design has an outline of black cross-stitches. Page 63 pictures it stitched onto a ready-made top.

Materials: 10" x 12" waste canvas
with 14 thread groups per inch;
a white T-shirt or top;
DMC embroidery threads listed.

Stitch count: 80H x 63W

Directions: Position the waste canvas on the front of the top, ensuring that it is squared up. Tack around the edges and diagonally so that the canvas is securely attached.

Stitch the design, using two strands of embroidery thread. When stitching is complete, remove the tacking threads, dampen the canvas with a cloth, and slowly pull out the strands of the waste canvas. Carefully press the finished garment.

	KEY for Paddington seated		
	DMC	Color	Stitches
■	310	black	1454
+	300	russet	737
○	422	light brown	1527
−	666	red	1171
×	797	blue	2574
∪	972	gold	71
•		white	159

Place Mat

Paddington's dreams of marmalade will brighten any breakfast table.

Materials: 8½" x 8½" cream Aida fabric
with 11 thread groups per inch;
DMC embroidery threads listed.

Stitch count: 53H x 53W

Directions: Stitch the design on the Aida fabric. Zigzag around the place mat, ½" in from each edge, using cream thread. Pull the threads of the Aida to form a ½" fringe. For extra durability, have the mat laminated.

KEY for Paddington dreaming			
	DMC	Color	Stitches
■	310	black	14
*	321	dark red	39
O	422	light brown	289
U	436	brown	31
+	444	yellow	287
×	666	red	952
−	740	orange	52
•	745	cream	30
	310	black	backstitch

	KEY for Paddington shopping		
	DMC	*Color*	*Stitches*
■	310	black	17
✳	321	dark red	69
O	422	light brown	277
Z	435	brown	64
•	648	gray	52
N	666	red	222
X	702	green	7
−	740	orange	75
<	745	cream	68
+	797	blue	588
U	972	gold	8
	310	black	backstitch

Shopping Bag

This handy bag, which features Paddington stocking up on his favorite delicacy, appears on page 70. For extra strength, line the bag with a waterproof material.

Materials: 24½" x 11" cream Aida fabric with 11 thread groups per inch; 28" of 1" wide cream tape; DMC embroidery threads listed.

Stitch count: 54H x 54W

Directions: Zigzag the edges of the Aida fabric to prevent fraying. Sew a 1" hem at both of the narrow ends. Stitch the design so that the top of the figure starts 3" below one of the hemmed edges. Press the stitched fabric carefully.

On each hemmed edge of the cloth, mark two points, each 3½" in from the sides. To form the handles, cut two pieces of the cream tape, each 14" long, and sew a 1" hem at each end. Pin each end of one length of

tape onto one of the hemmed edges at the two marked points. Sew around the overlap and diagonally so that the tape is attached securely to the bag. Repeat on the other hemmed edge.

Fold the fabric in half with the design face up and the two hemmed edges aligned. Pin the two layers of fabric at each side, at a point 2" up from the folded edge. Turn the front flap over and the bottom flap under so that the design is now inside the bag and there is a valley fold in the base. Sew a ½" seam along the two sides. Turn the completed bag inside out.

Diagram of Shopping Bag showing the folded Aida fabric with pins 2" up from the folded edge.

The bag with the front folded over and the back folded under to make a valley fold in the base.

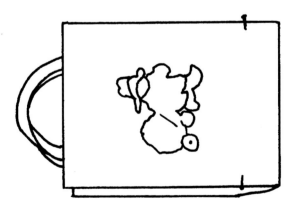

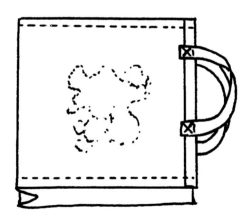

A small shopping bag is ideal for a small person. The instructions and chart for this design can be found on the previous pages.

PADDINGTON BEAR ™
© Paddington and Company Ltd 1995
Licensed by Copyrights

An apron is useful for cooking, craft-work, gardening, or any number of things. Instructions start on page 72.

	DMC	Color	Stitches
■	310	black	14
+	422	brown	298
×	666	red	596
N	703	green	54
✳	720	burnt orange	12
U	741	orange	155
O	797	blue	231
–	972	gold	27
	310	black	backstitch

KEY for Paddington gardening

Child's Apron

Paddington is one of those bears who like to be helpful but who inevitably create havoc. For some tasks, an apron, like the one shown on page 71, is indispensable.

Materials: 7" x 7" cream Aida fabric
with 11 thread groups per inch;
7" x 7" cream backing fabric;
22" x 22" colored fabric;
3¼ yards bias binding;
DMC embroidery threads listed.

Stitch count: 54H x 57W

Directions: Stitch the design on the Aida fabric and press the finished work. Back this with a square of light-colored fabric and trim the edges with bias binding: this section will be the apron pocket.

On a large piece of paper, draw the apron shape, using the pattern on the right as a guide. The height should be 22" and the half-width 9".

Fold the square of colored fabric in half and pin the paper pattern onto the fabric so that the dashed line is on the folded edge. Cut the fabric in the apron shape. Remove the pattern and zigzag the fabric edges to prevent fraying.

Sew a ½" hem on each straight edge. Pin a 7' piece of bias binding along the armhole curves to form a neck loop and apron ties. Make sure the ties are of even length. Starting at one tie end, sew the bias binding edges together, sew the bias binding around the armhole curves, and continue sewing to the other end of the tie.

Position the pocket on the front of the apron, 1½" from the top hem. With a cream thread, sew along the sides and base of the Aida fabric, securing the pocket in place.

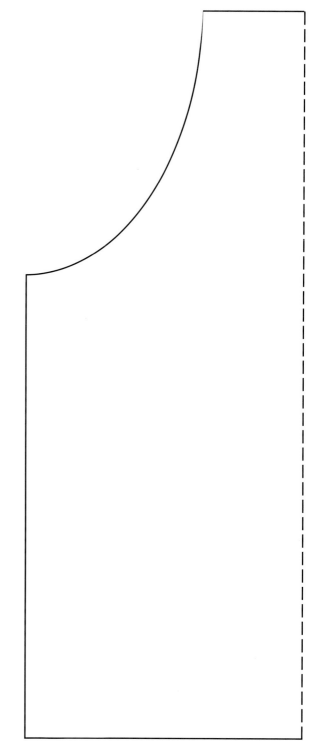

DUCK

Duck is featured in many books illustrated by Stephen Cartwright, including the best-selling First Thousand Words, in which he made his first appearance. Often he is discreetly hidden on the page for the eager child to discover, but occasionally he stars in his very own book (Find the Duck). He is really more duckling than duck, and small children delight in his playful and sometimes mischievous ways. A slight inclination of the beak, a minor adjustment of the dot-like eyes, and Duck bears a totally new expression. Duck's exploits are simple ones—going to the seaside, meeting up with new friends—but Cartwright's attention to detail makes every picture a story in itself. Indeed, the books are designed to encourage children to name objects and talk about actions while enjoying themselves. A relative new-comer to the world of children's books, Duck is fast becoming a great favorite with children and parents alike.

Duck and His Friends © Usborne Publishing Ltd. 1987

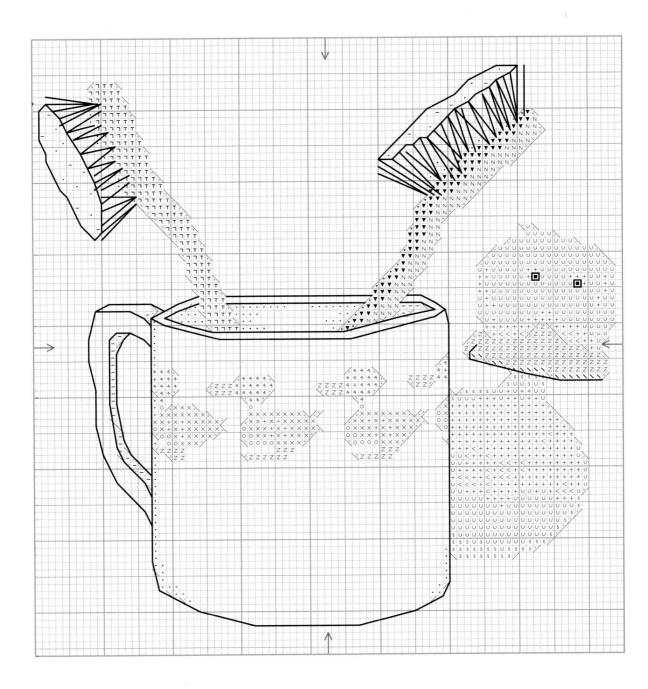

Wash Bag

Pictured on page 75 is a useful bag to take to nursery school or when visiting overnight at Grandma's house. To make it extra handy, you could line it with a waterproof material.

Materials: 8" x 8" white Aida fabric
with 14 thread groups per inch;
8" x 8" white backing fabric;
24" x 12" colored fabric;
28" strong cord;
DMC embroidery threads listed.

Stitch count: 78H x 84W

Directions: Stitch the design in the center of the Aida fabric and carefully press. Back with a piece of white fabric the same size. Cut four strips of colored fabric: a top panel and bottom panel each measuring 3" x 7", and two side panels each 2" x 10½". Cut a 10" x 9" piece for the back of the bag. Zigzag the edges of all pieces to prevent fraying.

Lay the top and bottom strips on the Aida with right sides facing and sew a ½" seam. Press seams flat and repeat with the side panels. Place the front and back sections together, right sides facing, and sew a ½" seam along the sides and base. Turn the neck of the bag over twice to create a casing deep enough for the cord. Sew the bottom of the casing, stopping ½" short of your starting point.

Attach a safety pin to one end of the cord and push it through the ½" gap and into the casing. Thread the cord around the casing and push it back out through the gap. Remove the pin. Tie the cord ends tightly.

KEY for Duck & toothbrushes			
	DMC	Color	Stitches
<	307	lemon	40
■	310	black	2
−	414	dark gray	59
•	415	light gray	127
+	444	yellow	281
×	517	teal	124
\	606	flame	21
Z	608	orange	138
⌐	666	red	95
4	701	dark green	66
O	704	light green	30
S	782	tan	58
▼	797	dark blue	93
N	798	blue	99
T	817	dark red	96
U	972	gold	345
Backstitch			
	817	dark red	mouth
	310	black	other details

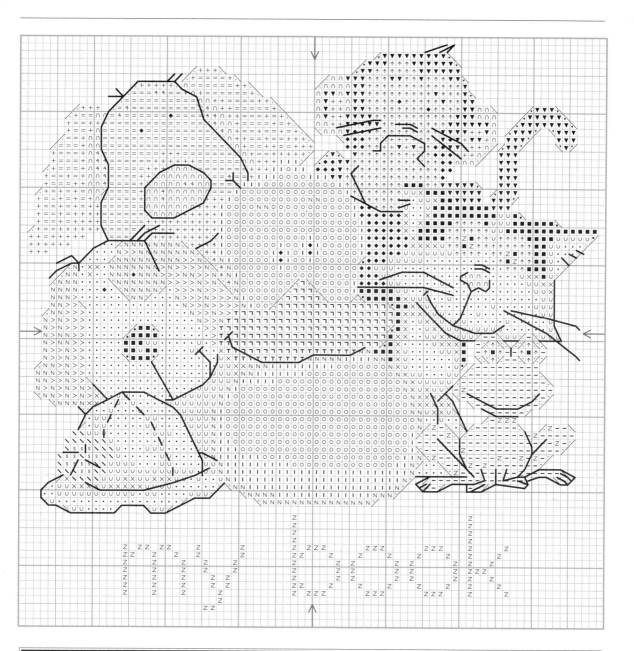

KEY for Cover		78H x 78W
DMC	Color	Stitches
▼ 300	brown	188
■ 310	black	132
∩ 353	apricot	125
> 400	red brown	98
4 407	mushroom	39
× 414	gray	88
∪ 415	light gray	280
○ 444	yellow	525
\ 601	crimson	28

DMC	Color	Stitches
s 604	pink	13
⌐ 606	orange	150
T 666	red	27
Z 701	green	138
↑ 745	pale yellow	235
+ 754	light peach	250
N 782	tan	228
− 907	lime green	251
◆ 938	dark brown	84
= 951	cream	294

DMC	Color	Stitches
I 972	gold	195
•	white	525

Backstitch

DMC	Color	
300	brown	monkey, duck
400	red brown	dog hairs
407	mushroom	pig
601	crimson	flower
701	green	frog
414	gray	other details

Cloth Book

This enchanting book opens to show each animal and its name. The designs are so sweet that you might reuse them in other projects.

Materials: 40" x 24" white Aida fabric with 14 thread groups per inch; thin white backing fabric; thin batting; green ribbon and sewing thread; DMC embroidery threads listed.

Directions: To make the full book, cut fourteen pieces of Aida fabric, each 8" square. On one square, stitch the cover design, which is shown on page 78. Then stitch each animal on a different square.

Stitch the name of each animal on an Aida square, using the chart on page 126.

Cut fourteen matching pieces of thin white backing fabric and back each Aida square with a piece. Cut seven matching pieces of thin batting. Construct each "page" with an animal on one side and a word on the other and a piece of batting in between. Make sure the sequence is correct so that facing pages match the name to the appropriate animal. Tack around the edges to secure the layers in place.

Zigzag the right-hand edge, top, and bottom with ¼" stitches in green thread. Repeat to create an edging of solid color. Bind the book by folding the left-hand edges of the cover and back page in between the center pages. Sew along the spine with a heavy-duty needle. Decorate with a ribbon.

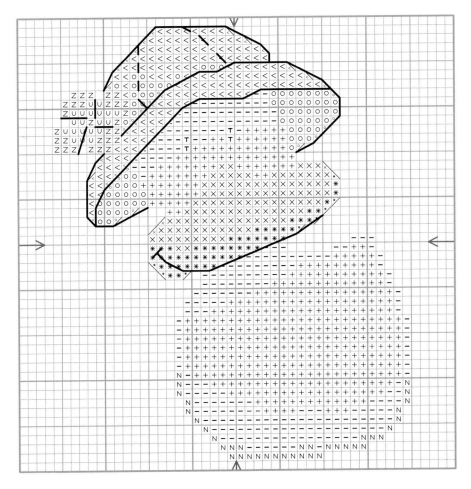

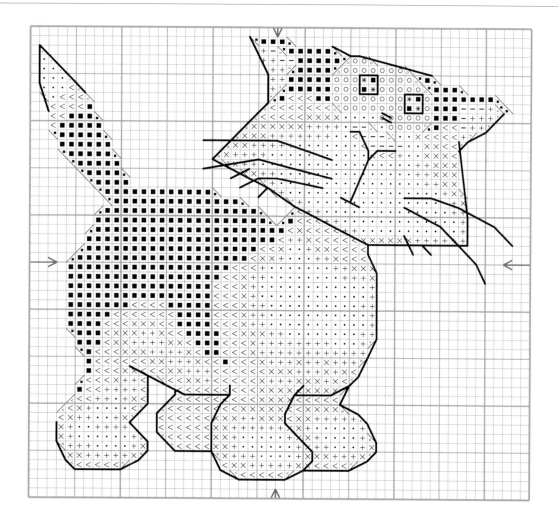

KEY for duck		48H x 41W
	DMC	Color	Stitches

	DMC	Color	Stitches
O	415	gray	93
+	444	yellow	410
Z	601	crimson	29
U	604	pink	20
X	606	orange	115
*	666	red	59
N	782	tan	38
T	938	brown	4
–	972	gold	250
<		white	168

Backstitch

	414	gray	hat
	601	crimson	flower
	938	brown	beak

KEY for cat		47H x 52W
	DMC	Color	Stitches

	DMC	Color	Stitches
■	310	black	390
–	353	apricot	21
<	413	dark gray	256
X	414	gray	175
+	415	light gray	230
*	701	green	4
O	745	cream	59
•		white	301
	310	black	backstitch

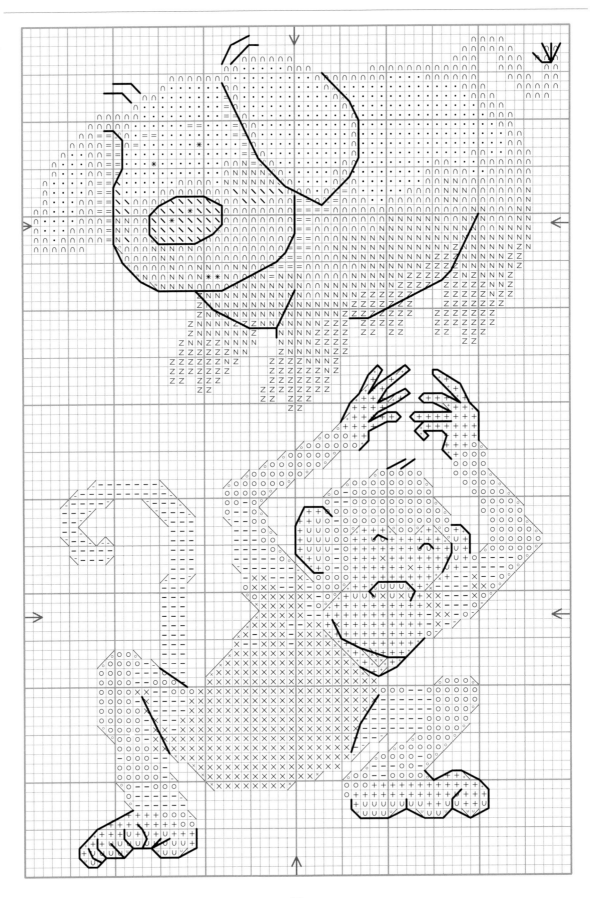

KEY for pig		40H x 58W	
	DMC	Color	Stitches
\	353	pink	48
=	407	mushroom	65
Z	452	light gray	182
N	453	dark gray	274
∩	754	apricot	451
✳	839	brown	6
•	951	cream	401
	839	brown	backstitch

KEY for monkey		53H x 53W	
	DMC	Color	Stitches
−	300	light brown	290
O	400	red brown	386
+	745	cream	260
×	898	brown	352
U	950	apricot	74
	898	brown	backstitch

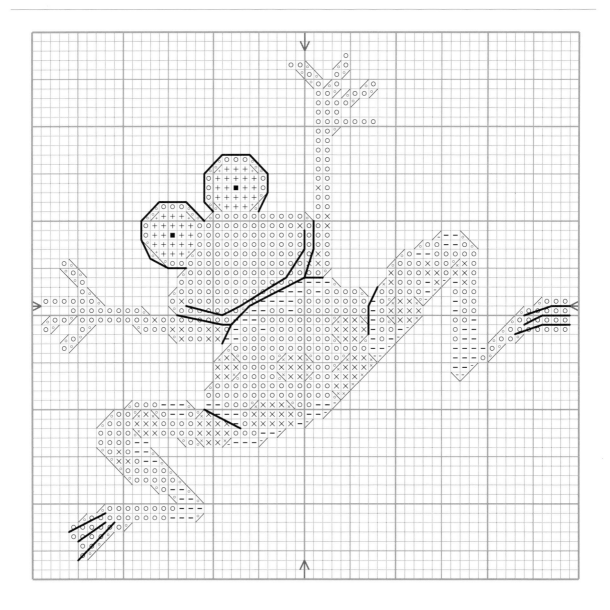

KEY for frog   54H x 58W

	DMC	Color	Stitches
■	310	black	2
✕	701	emerald	132
−	703	green	112
+	745	cream	48
○	907	lime green	629
	701	emerald	backstitch

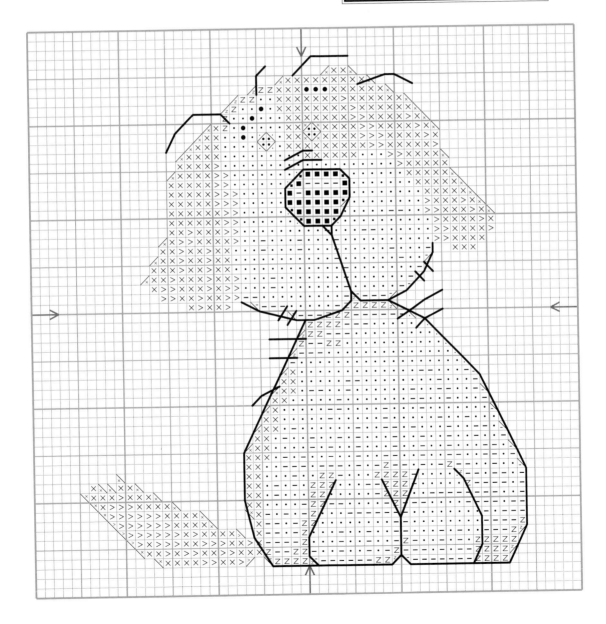

KEY for dog		53H x 49W
DMC	Color	Stitches
■ 310	black	33
Z 318	dark gray	91
> 400	brown	116
− 415	light gray	265
× 782	tan	367
● 938	dark brown	15
·	white	639

Backstitch

400	brown	head hairs
310	black	other detail

Growing Up

The school years
bring a range of exciting things to
learn and do. Here are lots of gifts
to make those years even more
enjoyable: small people will love
practicing the alphabet with Apple
Tree Farm, attending dance
classes with Angelina, and adven-
turing with Winnie-the-Pooh and
the ever-youthful Peter Pan.
Cross-stitch can be used to
decorate an infinite number of
things—pencil cases, sports bags,
T-shirts, beach towels—all of
which will appeal to older
children.

☆ ☆ PETER PAN ☆ ☆

Sir James Barrie was born in Scotland in 1860. His boyish imagination thrived on tales of desert islands, pirates, and Indian warriors as, with his friends, he played out many adventures. These images reappeared much later in many of his plays and stories. Barrie's own marriage was childless, but he formed close friendships with other people's children, in particular with the Llewellyn Davies family of five boys. In 1902 he wrote a story for the oldest boy entitled The Little White Bird, in which the character of Peter Pan first appeared. Later, when Barrie and his wife, Mary Ansell, bought a home in Surrey, the boys came to stay and played out the stories that Barrie so loved to tell them. From these shared adventures grew the world-famous play Peter Pan, which was first produced in London in December 1904. It made household names of such characters as Wendy, Tinker Bell, and the wicked Captain Hook. Peter Pan, the hero, is at times a little selfish and at others delightfully naive.

The boy who never grew up nonetheless grew in popularity and continues to live on in the hearts of children—of all ages.

KEY for Peter Pan			
	DMC	Color	Stitches
■	310	black	21
✳	610	brown	81
◯	701	dark green	296
✕	703	green	323
−	907	lime	149
•	928	smoke	368
∪	945	tan	219
+	948	light peach	389
<	3072	light smoke	347
▲	3712	pink	2

Backstitch
928	smoke	shadow
3371	chocolate	other details

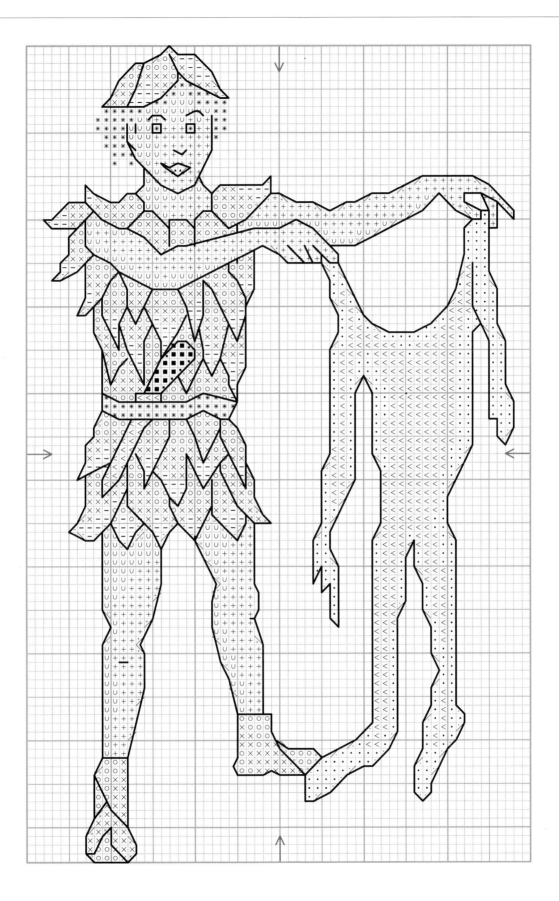

Pajama Case ☆ ☆ ☆

This design, pictured above, shows Peter with his shadow (before Wendy sews it back on).

Materials: 14" x 14" cream linen
with 30 threads per inch;
2 squares (14") backing fabric;
14" x 14" colored fabric;
Velcro® strips; ribbon;
DMC embroidery threads listed.

Stitch count: 94H x 56W

Directions: Stitch the design in the center of the linen. Zigzag all fabric pieces. Lay the stitched design face down on a backing square and sew a ½" seam along one edge. Turn inside out and press the seam. Sew the colored fabric and other backing square in the same way. Lay the two sections together with right sides facing and seamed edges aligned. Sew a ½" seam around the other three edges. Hand-sew strips of Velcro® onto either side of the opening. Turn the case inside out and press.

Album ☆ ☆ ☆ ☆ ☆ ☆ ☆ ☆ ☆ ☆

Tinker Bell, possibly the best-known fairy in the world, adorns this album cover. The pages, cut from colored card, could hold a collection of special photographs or cards.

Materials: 14" x 24" white linen
with 30 threads per inch;
sturdy white card;
thin colored card;
thin batting;
5' of narrow ribbon;
DMC embroidery threads listed.

Stitch count: 86H x 76W

Directions: Cut the linen into two pieces, each 14" x 12", and zigzag the edges. With the long edges as the top and bottom, stitch the design in the center of one of the linen rectangles. Carefully press the finished work.

Cut two pieces of card, each one 10½" x 8½". Mark a line 1½" in from the short edge on one piece and score it with a knife. Cut a piece of thin wadding 9" x 8½" and glue it onto the card, to the right of the scored line. Position the stitched work over the wadding, fold the edges over, and secure them with pins at the back. Lace the top and bottom with strong thread and then lace the two sides. Glue a piece of colored card over the lacing. With a sharp knife, make two cuts along the spine, each ½", in the same position as the holes created by a two-hole punch. Apply glue around the cuts to prevent the linen from fraying.

Make the back cover in the same way, but using the unstitched piece of linen. Cut pages of colored card ½" smaller than the covers and punch holes along one side.

	KEY for Tinker Bell		
	DMC	Color	Stitches
X	340	mauve	242
N	341	blue	533
+	369	green	179
*	402	bronze	79
Z	743	gold	14
−	945	light peach	115
<	948	apricot	109
U	3713	pink	210
O	3747	pale blue	540

Backstitch
301	brown	hair
340	mauve	dress & pupils
743	gold	stars & wandshine
3328	red	mouth
317	gray	other details

Cut a 20" length of ribbon and thread it through the slots in the back cover, the holes in the pages, and up through the front-cover slots. Tie the ribbon in a tight bow to bind the album securely.

Cut pieces of ribbon to form a frame on the front cover, cutting the ends at an angle to form mitered corners. Glue them in place on the linen. If the album will be handled often, you may wish to spray the covers with a protective coating.

 # ANGELINA

Angelina danced her way into children's hearts in the 1980's and has been making repeat curtain calls ever since. Her debut was suitably entitled Angelina Ballerina and was written by Katharine Holabird and illustrated by Helen Craig. It tells the tale of a young mouse who dreams of being a ballerina and, after causing a fair amount of havoc around the house, is given a present of ballet lessons by her parents, Mr. and Mrs. Mouseling. Angelina proved such a success that she twirled into many further adventures that introduced other family members, such as the delightful Cousin Henry. Helen Craig's fine illustrations are perfectly executed, endowing a white mouse with all the characteristics of a good-natured and excitable little girl. In a very short space of time, Holabird and Craig's widely acclaimed books have become contemporary classics for young readers.

Angelina™ Illustrations © Helen Craig 1983

Ballet Bag

This elegant drawstring bag can be used to hold ballet shoes, favorite slippers, or any personal treasures. The example on page 95 is made of multiple panels, but you could also appliqué the stitched design onto a finished bag.

Materials: 7" x 7" white Aida fabric with 14 thread groups per inch; 7" x 7" white backing fabric; 24" x 14" colored fabric; satin cord; DMC embroidery threads listed.

Stitch count: 55H x 48W

Directions: Stitch the design in the center of the Aida fabric. Back with a piece of white fabric cut to the same size. Zigzag the edges.

Cut four strips of colored fabric: a top panel measuring 7" x 3½", a bottom panel of 7" x 3", and two side panels each 2½" x 12½". Cut a piece for the back of the bag, 9½" x 12½". Zigzag the edges of all pieces to prevent fraying.

Lay the top and bottom strips on the Aida with right sides facing and sew a ½" seam. Press seams flat and repeat with the side panels. Place the front and back sections together, right sides facing, and sew a ½" seam along the sides and base. Turn the neck of the bag over twice to create a casing deep enough for the cord. Sew the bottom edge of the casing, stopping ½" short of your starting point.

Knot one end of the cord. Attach a safety pin to the other end of the cord and push it through the ½" gap and into the casing. Thread the cord around the casing and push it back out through the gap. Remove the pin and tie a knot in the end of the cord.

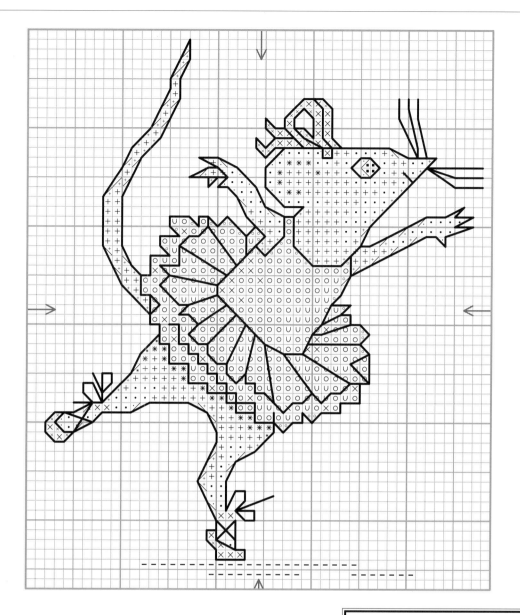

KEY for Angelina

	DMC	Color	Stitches
■	317	dark gray	4
*	318	gray	28
−	471	green	40
×	761	peach	72
+	762	light gray	197
U	819	pale pink	61
O	963	pink	281
•		white	118

Backstitch

317	dark gray	eye & mouth
318	gray	other details

Door Plate (page 100) and
Congratulations Card (page 101)

Angelina Baller

Doorplate

Angelina pirouettes her way into a slight faux pas in this charming design, shown on pages 98–99. If you wish to add a child's name, allow for extra fabric and card.

Materials: 20" x 10" white linen
with 27 threads per inch;
15" x 6" heavy white card stock;
narrow pink ribbon;
strong cotton thread;
DMC embroidery threads listed.

Stitch count: 33H x 173W

Directions: Zigzag the edges of the linen to prevent fraying. Stitch the design in the center of the linen, adding a name if desired. Carefully press the finished work.

Cut a sturdy piece of card and lay the stitched design over it, making sure it is straight. Fold the edges of the fabric over and secure it with pins at the back. Starting at the top left, lace the top and bottom edges

with strong thread. Repeat this with the two side edges.

Cut four pieces of ribbon: two 14" lengths and two 5" lengths. Cut the ends at an angle and glue the pieces onto the front of the panel to frame the design.

Attach another length of ribbon to the back of the panel for hanging the doorplate.

KEY for Angelina sequence			
	DMC	Color	Stitches
✱	318	gray	55
✕	761	dark pink	257
U	762	light gray	410
O	819	pale pink	46
+	963	pink	602
•		white	70
	317	dark gray backstitch	

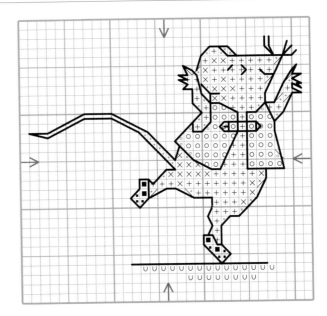

KEY for Henry		
DMC	Color	Stitches
O 307	yellow	50
■ 317	gray	11
U 772	green	24
X 841	fawn	30
+ 842	mushroom	106

Backstitch
310	black	eye & mouth
317	gray	shoes, pin & ground
839	brown	other details

Congratulations Card

Henry hasn't quite learned the finer details of dance, but he tries hard. Here is a lovely card for a child who has achieved or simply made an attempt.

Materials: 5½" x 5½" white Aida fabric with 14 thread groups per inch; 15" x 5" cream card stock; double-sided tape; ribbon; DMC embroidery threads listed.

Stitch count: 26H x 30W

Directions: Stitch the design on the Aida. On one side of the cream card, lightly score two lines and fold, creating three even panels. Use a compass to pencil a 1½"-radius circle in the center panel and cut it out with a sharp knife. Apply double-sided tape on the inside of the window and place the stitched work so that it shows through. Tape down the left-hand panel. With the compass, emboss a circle ¼" outside the window. Decorate with a ribbon.

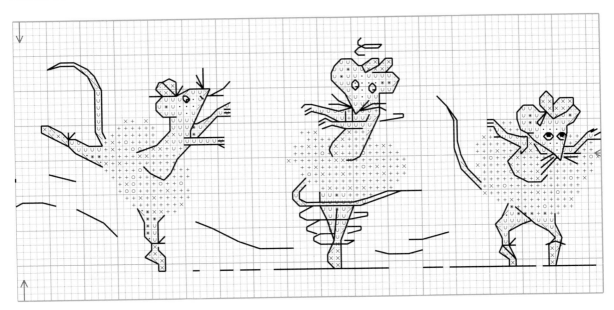

APPLE TREE FARM

This chapter contains a whole cast of popular characters: the creatures who live at Apple Tree Farm. Farmyard Tales is a collection of delightful stories written by Heather Amery and illustrated by Stephen Cartwright. Each story has been written for children who are just beginning to read and recounts the adventures of Mrs. Boot, the farmer; her children, Poppy and Sam; and their dog, Rusty. The stories re-create the daily chores and activities of life on a farm (something of a mystery to city children) in a gentle and humorous way. A day for the Boot family is never dull. A lost piglet, a runaway tractor, a prizewinning donkey—there is always some excitement. The many animals are the real stars of the show, as Stephen Cartwright endows each one with distinctive and quirky characteristics. Duck, featured earlier in this book, is another charming inhabitant of Apple Tree Farm.

Apple Tree Farm © Usborne Publishing Ltd 1991

Alphabet Sampler 🍎 🍎

This charming alphabet can be stitched as a complete sampler or as individual letters. There are no half-stitches in the designs, making them ideal for those just learning to cross-stitch.

Materials: 30" x 30" white Aida fabric with 14 thread groups per inch; DMC embroidery threads listed.

Stitch count: 273H x 273W

Directions: Tack one thread across the Aida fabric and another from top to bottom, marking the center of the fabric. Stitch the letter "K," which is in the center of the design, and then work out from there. The diagram below indicates how the charts fit together.

When all the letters are completed, add a red border one stitch wide around the whole design. Carefully press the finished work and have it professionally framed.

	p.105	p.106	p.107
	p.109	p.112	p.113

KEY for alphabet sampler

	DMC	Color	Stitches
/	224	pink	40
◆	300	russet	377
∴	301	rust	291
■	310	black	176
▲	334	gray-blue	614
Z	407	fawn	541
✳	414	gray	761
→	415	light gray	477
H	436	light brown	112
↑	444	yellow	464
T	469	dark green	209
−	471	green	996
O	606	flame	477
⁒	647	gray-green	332
X	666	red	3310
<	677	straw	359
>	734	olive	237
N	740	orange	206
F	780	dark tan	262
4	782	light tan	138
\	798	dark blue	274
●	839	mud	288
⊡	840	mushroom	391
+	945	light peach	239
I	950	peach	403
∩	972	gold	299
S	977	bronze	573
U	3042	mauve	314
=	3072	silver	773
≠	3328	rose	188
•		white	389

Backstitch

407	fawn	arm & chin of F
414	gray	J, M, body of Z
839	mud	D, G, pig in P
310	black	other details

	DMC	Color	Stitches
/	224	pink	40
◆	300	russet	377
∴	301	rust	291
■	310	black	176
▲	334	gray-blue	614
Z	407	fawn	541
✳	414	gray	761
→	415	light gray	477
H	436	light brown	112
↑	444	yellow	464
T	469	dark green	209
—	471	green	996
O	606	flame	477
⁒	647	gray-green	332
X	666	red	3310
<	677	straw	359
>	734	olive	237
N	740	orange	206
F	780	dark tan	262
⊦	782	light tan	138
＼	798	dark blue	274
●	839	mud	288
⊡	840	mushroom	391
+	945	light peach	239
I	950	peach	403
∩	972	gold	299
ς	977	bronze	573
U	3042	mauve	314
=	3072	silver	773
≠	3328	rose	188
•		white	389

KEY for alphabet sampler

Backstitch
407	fawn	arm & chin of F
414	gray	J, M, body of Z
839	mud	D, G, pig in P
310	black	other details

The Farm Alphabet

A is for apple tree
B is for barn
C is for chicken
D is for dog
E is for eggs
F is for farmer
G is for goat
H is for horse
I is for ivy
J is for jumper
K is for kitten
L is for lamb
M is for mouse
N is for nest
O is for owl
P is for pig
Q is for quack
R is for rabbits
S is for scarecrow
T is for tractor
U is for umbrella
V is for vegetables
W is for wheelbarrow
X is for ten apples
Y is for yellow
Z is for sleeping soundly.

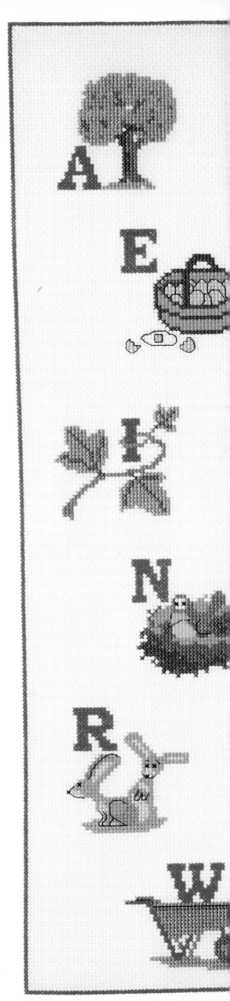

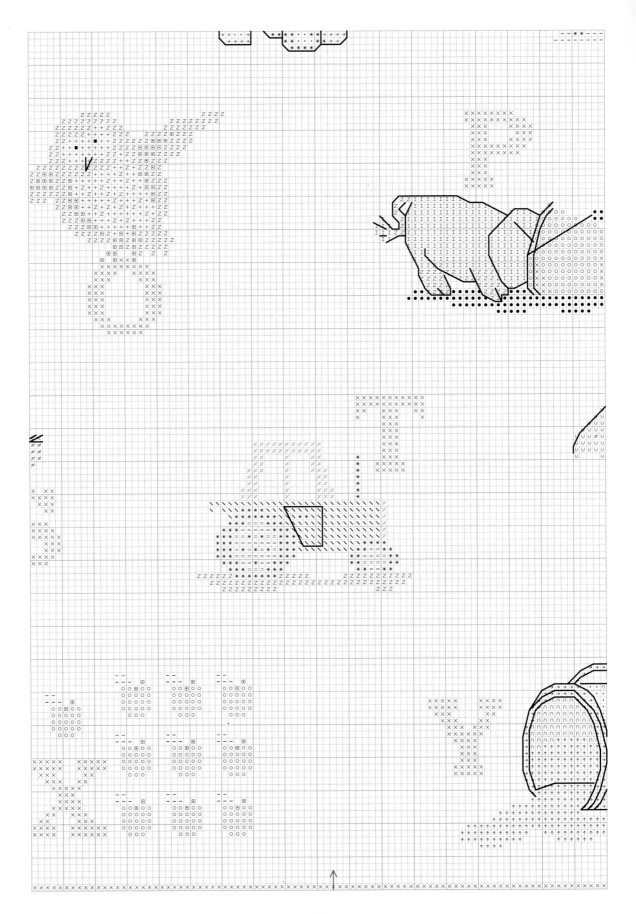

WINNIE-THE-POOH

This Bear of Little Brain is arguably the most famous and best-loved bear in the world. What he lacks in common sense is more than made up for in generosity, ingenuity, and a talent for composing hums. Pooh is the brilliant offspring of A. A. Milne, a successful playwright and novelist who turned his hand to writing poetry for children one rainy holiday in Wales. The result, When We Were Very Young (1924), was illustrated perfectly by Ernest H. Shepard and published to great acclaim. That volume featured an unnamed teddy bear. Milne followed this up with a storybook specifically about Pooh and his friends: Winnie-the-Pooh (1926). Now We Are Six (1927), another collection of verse, included Pooh. It was followed in 1928 by a second storybook, The House At Pooh Corner. The books also feature Milne's own son, Christopher Robin, whose stuffed animals served as inspiration for the inhabitants of the forest. The world can't be grateful enough for Winnie-the-Pooh, Piglet, Eeyore, Tigger, and the others who live in and around the Hundred Acre Wood.

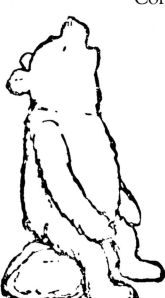

KEY for Pooh's friends

	DMC	Color	Stitches
■	310	black	16
✳	317	dark gray	33
O	318	light gray	201
Z	435	brown	27
▬	642	gray brown	97
⌐	700	green	17
+	721	orange	113
N	782	dark gold	23
U	783	gold	135
X	3772	red brown	89
S	3774	mushroom	42
•		white	208
	310	black	backstitch

Photocopying of Winnie-the-Pooh designs for sale
is strictly prohibited by law.

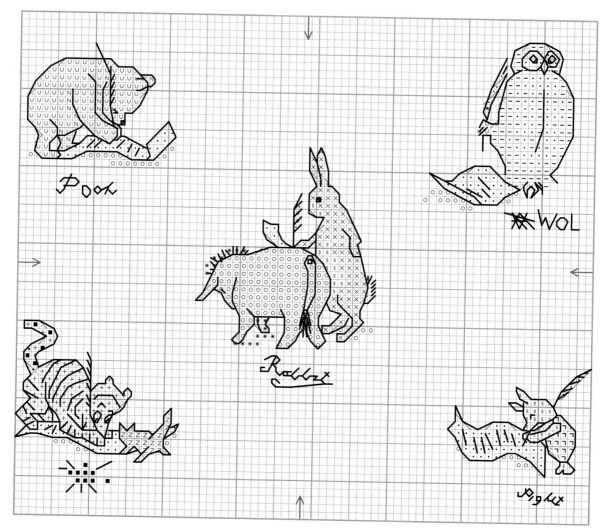

Autograph Book

Start off an autograph collection with a few signatures from Winnie-the-Pooh and his friends. The measurements given are for covering a 5" x 6½" album and may need to be adjusted if another size is used.

Materials: 8" x 16" white linen
with 26 threads per inch;
a small autograph album;
6" x 14" thin batting;
double-sided tape;
DMC embroidery threads listed.

Stitch count: 60H x 77W

Directions: Fold the fabric in half so that the short edges are together and lie on the right. Stitch the design in the center of the top panel. Press the finished work and zigzag the edges to prevent fraying.

Stick down double-sided tape around the edges of the album's cover. Wrap a piece of batting around the album, trimming it at the edges to fit the cover.

Lay the padded album onto the stitched work so that the design is centered on the front cover. Secure the short edges of the linen inside each cover with double-sided tape. Snip at an angle along the top and bottom of the linen where the spine of the album falls. Fold the V-shaped sections under so that they lie between the batting and the linen cover.

Turn one corner of the linen in and then fold the flap over and secure it inside the cover with double-sided tape. Repeat for each corner.

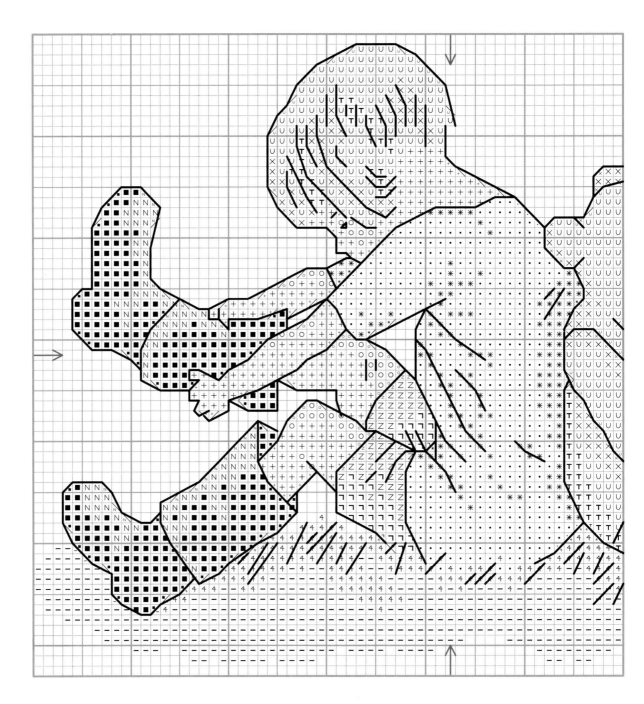

Framed Picture

On pages 118–119, Christopher Robin and Pooh prepare to discover the North Pole. The Expotition is a great success, as will the picture be when presented to an adventurous child.

Materials: 18" x 14" white linen with 25 threads per inch; white board or heavy card stock; DMC embroidery threads listed.

Stitch count: 61H x 85W

Directions: Stitch the design in the center of the fabric and press the work carefully. Cut strong white board to a suitable size. Lay the work over the board and make sure that it is centered. Fold the edges of the fabric around the board and use a strong thread to lace the edges together— side to side and top to bottom.

Fit the covered board into a ready-made frame or have it professionally framed.

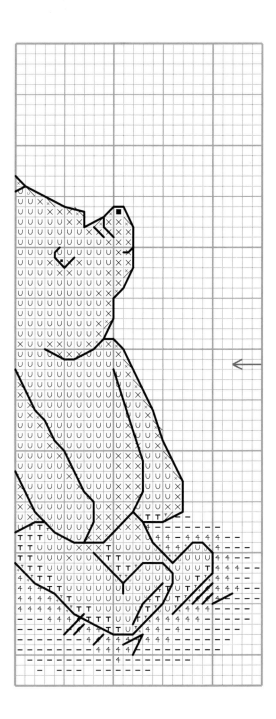

KEY - Christopher Robin & Pooh			
	DMC	Color	Stitches
■	310	black	323
N	317	dark gray	113
*	318	light gray	148
Z	350	coral	57
4	702	dark green	240
−	704	light green	508
O	754	peach	61
T	780	dark gold	115
X	782	gold	254
U	783	pale gold	659
⌐	817	red	46
+	948	mushroom	249
•		white	455
	310	black	backstitch

Pillowcase

Pooh and Piglet are the best sort of company at bedtime, when there is a great deal to think about and consider.

Materials: 6" x 6" waste canvas
with 14 thread groups per inch;
a cream cotton pillowcase;
DMC embroidery threads listed.

Stitch count: 50H x 63W

Directions: Position the waste canvas in the top right of the pillowcase, near the opening. Tack around the edges and also diagonally so that the canvas is securely attached to one layer of the pillowcase.

Stitch the design, then remove tacking threads. Dampen the canvas with a cloth and carefully pull out the strands.

KEY for Pooh & Piglet			
	DMC	Color	Stitches
■	310	black	4
<	754	pale peach	220
▲	898	chocolate	147
⌐	910	dark green	101
Z	913	pale green	273
U	948	cream	641
×	976	dark tan	200
−	977	tan	163
+	3341	dark peach	265
•	3824	peach	390
O	3827	light tan	76
	310	black	backstitch

These alphabets and numbers can be used to personalize many projects in this book.

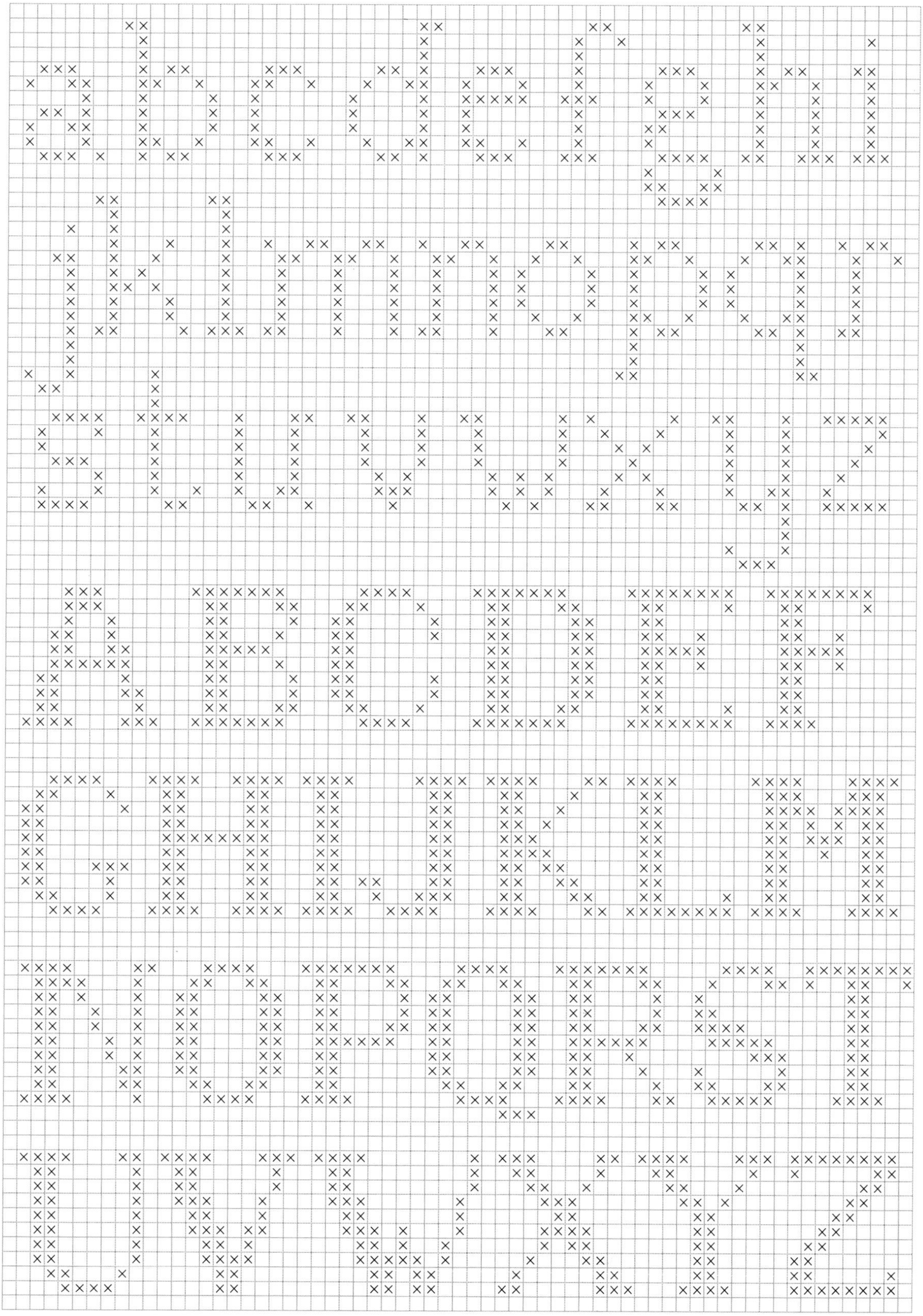

Below: Design for Height Chart (page 40).

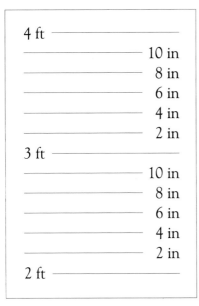

4 ft	
	10 in
	8 in
	6 in
	4 in
	2 in
3 ft	
	10 in
	8 in
	6 in
	4 in
	2 in
2 ft	

Below: Chart for the Cloth Book (page 80). Stitch each animal name in the center of a fabric "page."

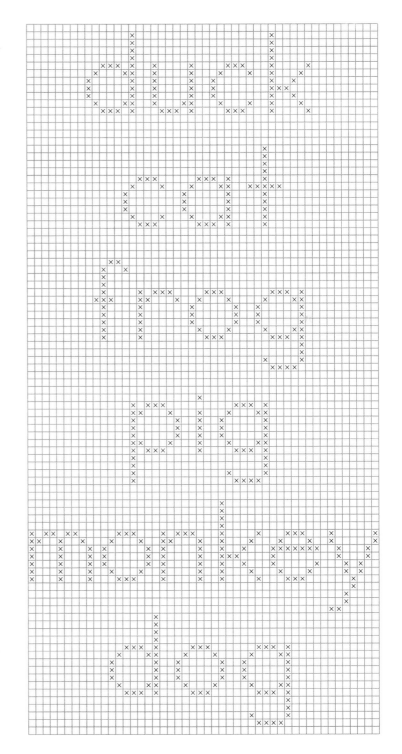

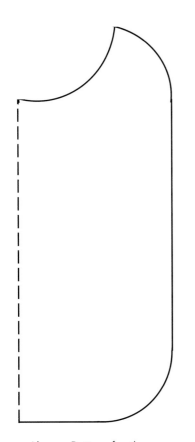

Above: Pattern for the
Feeding Bib (page 45).

ACKNOWLEDGMENTS

The charts in this book were created with StitchCraft, a Windows-based software program for designing counted charts. For information on this program, please contact Crafted Software in Australia or its U.S. distributor:
Crafted Software, PO Box 78, Wentworths Falls NSW 2782, Australia.   Fax: 011 61 47 573337
or Stitchdesign, 5523 South 700 West, Murray, Utah 84123, USA. Tel & Fax: 801 269 1948

Madeline designs and illustrations are drawn from *Madeline* and *Madeline and the Bad Hat*, by Ludwig Bemelmans. Copyright 1939 by Ludwig Bemelmans, renewed © 1967 by Madeleine Bemelmans and Barbara Bemelmans Marciano. Used by permission of Viking Penguin, a division of Penguin Books USA Inc.

The Beatrix Potter designs are based on illustrations from *The Tale of Peter Rabbit* and *The Tale of Mrs. Tiggy-Winkle*, by Beatrix Potter. Line drawings are from *The Peter Rabbit and Benjamin Bunny Colouring Book*. Copyright © Frederick Warne & Co., 1902, 1905, 1992, 1995.

Babar and the distinctive likeness thereof are trademarks of Laurent de Brunhoff and are used with his permission, and courtesy of Nelvana Limited and The Clifford Ross Company, Ltd. Copyright © Laurent de Brunhoff. All rights reserved.

The Spot designs are based on illustrations from *Where's Spot?* and *My Very Own Spot Book*. Line drawings are from *My Very Own Spot Book*. Copyright © Eric Hill/Salspot, 1980, 1993, 1995.

Miffy and other illustrations by Dick Bruna, © Mercis b.v.

Paddington Bear ™ © Paddington and Company Ltd 1995. Licensed by Copyrights.

Duck designs and illustrations are taken from *Find the Duck* and *Duck and His Friends*, illustrated by Stephen Cartwright and published by Usborne Publishing Ltd.

Angelina books are published by ABC, The All Children's Company Limited.

Apple Tree Farm designs and illustrations are taken from *Farmyard Tales*, illustrated by Stephen Cartwright and published by Usborne Publishing Ltd.

With grateful thanks to the Walt Disney Company for the inclusion of Classic Pooh™ designs, based on the Winnie-the-Pooh works. Copyright © A. A. Milne and E. H. Shepard. Winnie-the-Pooh designs and illustrations are taken from *Winnie-the-Pooh* and *The House At Pooh Corner*, by A. A. Milne, illustrated by E. H. Shepard. Copyrights 1926 and 1928 by E. P. Dutton, renewed © 1954 and 1956 by A. A. Milne. Used by permission of Dutton Children's Books, a division of Penguin Books USA Inc.

Special thanks to those who helped to stitch the designs: Maryse Pedersen, Judy Chambers, Mary Kuitert, Jennifer Kuitert, and Joanna Simpson.

The author is also grateful to DMC for fabrics and embroidery threads used throughout.

INDEX

746.443 $19.95
Sou   Souter, Gillian
       Storybook
     favorites in
     cross-stitch